STRENGTHS of Their OWN

Dedication

To my wife Betsy for her faithful and ardent love that she showers upon me, her sacrificial support of me and my work, and her tender care for our seven children to whom she is a continual blessing.

STRENGTHS of Their OWN

HOME SCHOOLERS ACROSS AMERICA

ACADEMIC ACHIEVEMENT, FAMILY CHARACTERISTICS, & LONGITUDINAL TRAITS

Brian D. Ray, Ph.D.

Strengths of Their Own
Home Schoolers Across America
Academic Achievement, Family
Characteristics, and Longitudinal Traits

Copyright © 1997 by Brian D. Ray
All Rights Reserved

Published by:
NHERI Publications
National Home Education Research Institute
PO Box 13939
925 Cottage Street NE
Salem, Oregon 97309 U.S.A.
   tel. (503) 364-1490
   facsimile (503) 364-2827
   World Wide Web Site http://www.nheri.org
   e-mail: mail@nheri.org

Library of Congress Catalog Card Number (LCCN): 97-91643
International Standard Book Number (ISBN): 0-9657554-0-1
Cover design by Jeff Sharpton, DesignPoint, Inc.
Printed in the United States of America by Morris Publishing,
   Kearney, Nebraska

Table of Contents

PREFACE   ix

ACKNOWLEDGMENTS   x

ABOUT THE AUTHOR   xi

ABSTRACT   xii

INTRODUCTION TO THE STUDY   1

Purpose of the Study   2

Review of Literature and Conceptual Framework   3

America's Educational Context   4

Concerns of Education Professionals   5

Research on Learner Outcomes   7

METHODOLOGY   15

The Instrument   15

Definitions   16

Population and Sample   17

Pilot Study   19

Distribution and Collection of the Instrument, and

    Response Rate   19

Data Entry, Data Analysis, and Statistical Hypotheses   21

Assumptions   24

Delimitations and Limitations   25

FINDINGS   27

Family Characteristics   27

Children's Characteristics   45

Students' Academic Achievement   54

Graduates of Home Education   67

Longitudinal Findings   68

CONCLUSIONS AND COMMENTARY   71

Families   71

Children   74

Graduates of Home Education   82

Longitudinal Findings   83

Strengths of Home Education   85

Closing Remarks   102

APPENDICES   103

REFERENCES   127

INDEX   141

Preface

Home schooling has clearly caught the imagination of the American public as we approach the 21st century. Whether it is called home schooling, homeschooling, home education, home-based education, or home-centered learning, this age-old practice has experienced a rebirth and taken hold in every state of the Union.

This book, based on the findings of my second nationwide study of home education in the United States, touches upon a wide range of topics. I address the basic demographic characteristics of home school families, the academic achievement of the home educated, selected policy issues related to home schooling, and selected traits of hundreds of families who were also studied about a half decade earlier. Relatively in-depth analysis is offered on some topics while only cursory attention is given to others. I invite other researchers to further explore those areas that need more attention.

Although advocates and critics of conventional schools (e.g., the common state-controlled, that is, public, and private schools that exist in the United States) are constantly searching for pedagogical methods and management strategies that will improve schools or trying to show that they are hopelessly ineffective, this study mainly offers descriptive and correlational statistics regarding home education. The findings and multivariate analyses, however, may evoke theorizing about causative factors with respect to the academic achievement of the home educated compared to that of students in conventional schools. That is, perhaps there *is* something intrinsic about home schooling that causes high academic achievement.

I am confident that in this treatise I have answered many questions about home schooling. Simultaneously, I am sure that my treatment of certain topics will serve to raise questions and stimulate some readers to articulate cautions about my conclusions (or about what certain readers may infer are my implied claims). I look forward to further friendly conversation and debate about my findings, inferences, and conclusions.

— Brian D. Ray, Ph.D.   April, 1997

Acknowledgments

I am grateful for the help of many in this project. The research could only be done with the cooperation of home education families across America. I received special assistance from Dr. Gregory Cizek of the University of Toledo (Ohio), Dr. Douglas Kelley of Arizona State University West, Dr. James Carper of the University of South Carolina, William Lloyd of the United States Bureau of the Census and Computer Reclamation, and Christopher Klicka of the Home School Legal Defense Association in terms of reviewing the methodology and preparation of this final report. I am especially thankful for the diligent assistance and encouragement of William Lloyd through many other aspects of this project. Michael and Joanie Tindall have also been an excellent help during this study. Karen Langsather gave me excellent assistance, upon short notice, in preparing the final manuscript. Several persons helped with data entry and other clerical duties; I especially want to thank Hallie Ray and Rachel Ray. My wife and my children were especially loving and understanding, as they are typically, during several phases of this project—they are a continual and rich blessing from the LORD. I am heartily appreciative of all of these people. I am very grateful to the Home School Legal Defense Association for sponsoring this study. I am also thankful to the National Home Education Research Institute and all those who support the institute; they were an essential part of making this research possible. I praise and thank the one and only true God — the LORD God who has revealed Himself through His creation and the Bible, that is, the Father, Son, and Holy Spirit — who loves me, has saved me, guides me in all ways, and provides for all my needs. —B.D.R.

About the Author

Brian D. Ray is president of the National Home Education Research Institute (Salem, Oregon, U.S.A.) and holds an earned Ph.D. in science education from Oregon State University (Corvallis, Oregon, U.S.A.). He is the founding (est. 1985) editor of the quarterly, refereed (juried), research journal, *Home School Researcher* (ISSN 1054-8033). Dr. Ray has served as a professor at the undergraduate and graduate levels at colleges and universities in the areas of research methodology, science, education, and statistics,. He has also taught at the elementary and secondary levels in public and private schools. Dr. Ray has conducted numerous studies and regularly publishes in scholarly journals and books, has presented numerous papers at professional meetings (e.g., of the American Educational Research Association, Association for Supervision and Curriculum Development, and National Association of State Boards of Education), appears as an expert witness in court cases, testifies to legislatures, appears in the news media, and speaks at a number of public conferences on the topic of home education. He is considered a leading expert on home education both in the United States and internationally.

Abstract

The purpose of this nationwide study was to examine the academic achievement and social activities of home educated students and the basic demographics of their families, to assess the relationships between student achievement and selected student and family variables, and to describe and explore certain longitudinal changes among home educated students and their families.

The target population was all home schooling families in the United States. Data were collected on 1,657 families and their 5,402 children—275 of the families participated in the author's 1990 study.

These families, with 3.3 children and 98% being headed by married couples, were much larger than the United States average. Ninety-five percent of family income was earned by the fathers; 34% of them were professionals and 11% were small business owners. Eighty-eight percent of the mothers were homemakers/home educators and only 16% of the mothers worked outside the home. A wide variety of religious affiliations was evident; about 90% of the parents were Christians. The parents had higher than average educational attainment; 46% of the fathers had a bachelor's degree or higher and 42% of the mothers had the same. These families' median annual income of $43,000 was a little lower than the median for all married-couple families in the United States. The parents spent, on average, $546 per child per year for home education.

The mother did 88% of the formal teaching of the children while the father did 10% of the teaching. The large majority of these children were not being taught by professionally trained and government certified teachers.

On average, the children had been taught at home for 5 years since age 5, 85% were in grades K through 8, and their parents planned to home educate them through their secondary school years. Parents hand picked curriculum materials—rather than purchasing complete programs—for 71% of the students. The social activities of these children were quite varied; for example, 47%

were involved in music classes, 48% were involved in group sports, and 77% participated in Sunday school.

These students scored, on the average, at high percentiles on standardized academic achievement tests: (a) total reading, 87th, (b) total language, 80th, (c) total math, 82nd, (d) total listening, 85th, (e) science, 84th, (f) social studies, 85th, (g) study skills, 81st, (h) basic battery (typically, reading, language, and mathematics), 85th, and (i) complete battery (all subject areas in which student was tested), 87th. (The national average is the 50th percentile.)

Several analyses were conducted to determine which independent variables were significantly related to academic achievement. There was *no* significant relationship between achievement and (a) whether the father was a certified teacher, (b) whether the mother was a certified teacher, (c) family income, (d) money spent on education, (e) legal status of the family, (f) time spent in formal instruction, (g) age formal instruction began, and (h) degree of state regulation of home schooling.

Achievement was statistically significantly related, in some cases, to father's education level, mother's education level, gender of student, years home educated, use of libraries, who administered the test, and use of computers. The relationships were, however, weak and not practically significant.

This and other studies indicate that very few background variables (e.g., socioeconomic status of parents, regulation by the state) explain the academic achievement of the home educated. It is possible that the home education environment ameliorates the effect of variables that are typically considered a detriment to students. A variety of students in a variety of home education settings have performed very well in terms of academic achievement.

1

Introduction to the Study

Effective educational approaches have been ever-elusive since professional educators, compulsory attendance laws, and state-controlled schools grew ubiquitous in America during the late 1800s. Many people have reported on changes in education and schooling and the search for schools that effectively teach children (Blumenfeld, 1984, p. 37; Duffy, 1995; Hirsch, 1996; Lieberman, 1993; National Commission on Excellence in Education, 1983; Perelman, 1992; Sowell, 1993; Toch,1991b; Tyack, 1974). One explanation for the elusiveness of effectiveness is that before the 1900s maybe no one was interested in evaluating the state of education nationwide. Or, it may be that professional educators and government schools caused effective approaches to become extinct. A third explanation may be that an effective educational approach was nonexistent before the late 1800s and is simply yet to be discovered and implemented. Regardless of the true cause of failure to arrive at successful education for the masses in the United States, hundreds of thousands of parents have decided to not wait for professional educators and government-controlled schools to serve their children. These parents have literally taken the education of their children into their own hands—they home educate them.

There are an estimated 700,000 to 1,150,000 home schooled children in grades kindergarten through 12 during the 1996-1997 academic year (Clark, 1994; Lines, 1991, 1996; Ray, 1996). Although dependable estimates are difficult to attain, the growth rate appears to be at least 15% per year (Ray, 1996). If these numbers are accurate, 1 to 2 percent of children are currently home educated. If these numbers are accurate and the 15% growth rate holds true, there could be 2.3 million or more home schooled children by the 2003-2004 academic year — 4% or more of the school-aged population (United States Department of Education, Office of Educational Research and Improvement, 1993). Michael Farris, president of the Home School Legal Defense Association, once thought that the home education population would never exceed a clear minority of the school-aged population. Based on his recent experiences, advances in technology, public opinion about and the use of distance learning, and changes in society, Farris (1996) recently said:

> Well, many of us have believed for a long time that home schooling would max out around about five to seven percent of the population. I have said that for many years. I withdraw that assessment . . . I see a day, and I believe I am going to live to see the day, where nearly half of American children will be home schooled for at least a significant portion of their academic training.

Either scenario—2 to 3 million children in 2003-2004 or nearly 50% of all children within a generation learning in home-based education—is a staggering change from the 89% in state-run schools today (United States Department of Education, Office of Educational Research and Improvement, 1993). Change breeds questions and doubts? The question has been asked, and continues to be asked: "What effect does home education have on children's learning, children's psychological and social development, and upon society as a whole?"

Purpose of the Study

The research base on home education has expanded dramatically since the first studies and academic articles of the late 1970s that dealt with the modern home education movement. Numerous researchers have examined learner outcomes such as academic achievement, psychological and social development, and psychomotor development; and they have explored various other aspects and issues related to home education in disciplines such as philosophy, sociology, and law. Very few studies, however, have studied a nationwide population of home educators and their children. Even fewer, if any, have studied a nationwide sample over the course of half a decade.

The purpose of this nationwide study is to examine the academic achievement and social activities of home educated students and the basic demographics of their families, to assess the relationships between student achievement and selected student and family variables, and to describe and explore certain longitudinal changes among home educated students and their families.

Review of Literature and Conceptual Framework

Home schooling is now a stable and fast-growing form of education in America. Home education is also rapidly reemerging in other developed nations around the world (Bendell, 1987; Ray, 1994; Webb, 1990). Whereas the home has often been the predominant center of education throughout the history of western civilization (Common & MacMullen, 1986; Gordon & Gordon, 1990), many countries shifted to the elaborate institutionalization of education during the late 19th and 20th centuries. The practice of children being taught at home by tutors, nannies, and parents, however, has never totally disappeared. Klicka (1993) and Common and MacMullen (1986) pointed out, for example, that Winston Churchill, Agatha Christie, Abraham Lincoln, Jamie and Andrew Wyeth, and C.S. Lewis were all home schooled as children. And during the past 20 years, there has been a dramatic increase in the number of parents who have decided to be the primary educators in their children's lives rather than send them away to schools to be taught by other adults. The home has once again clearly become the most meaningful center of activity and learning for these children.

In spite of critics who say that these children will not be prepared for life in this highly technological age, these parents claim that with their own skills, their love for their children, and the aid of modern technology (e.g., computers, modems, video courses, and on-line services such as the *Internet*) they can provide a solid education for their children (Breshears, 1996, p. 83-88; Churbuck, 1993; Stecklow, 1994).

America's Educational Context

These parents' decision to home educate their children might not be very surprising if one were to consider recent developments in American education. It appears that little has settled down since the famous *A Nation At Risk* report was published in 1983 (National Commission on Excellence in Education). The report described America's government-run schools to be in such an inferior state of being and their students learning so little that it was as if the United States had declared war on itself. Since then, there have been nationwide educational battles over back-to-basics curriculum, school choice and the privatization of schooling, school vouchers, charter schools, the need (if any) for institutionalized schools, the government's role (if any) in teaching and raising children, moral education, outcome-based education (OBE), and national curriculum and achievement standards (see, e.g., Buehrer, 1995; Donmoyer, 1996; Duffy, 1995; Hudson, 1992, 1993; Lieberman, 1989; 1993; Martin, 1992; Nash, 1990; Perelman, 1992; Sowell, 1993; Toch, 1991b) The educational-political scene has been turbulent for over a decade. It appears, to date, that the debates and the proposing of solutions will not soon cease.

While the government, professional educators, and politicians are devising strategies for improvement, many parents today are not willing to wait for change in public schools while their children are in them and affected by them (Toch, 1991a). While many are moving toward private schools, there has also been a quiet, but significant, migration to home education. Whether the motivation is "the positive entry [to home education] impulse" or "the negative exit [from institutionalized schools] impulse" (Audain, 1987, p. 18), many parents are choosing home education as an alternative to both government and private schools (Lewis, 1985). Home education appears to be here to stay.

Estimates of the number of home educated students are difficult to develop (Lines, 1991). Recent estimates by researchers place the number from just over 500,000 to 1.15 million children in grades K through 12 for the 1996-1997 academic year (Lines, 1996; Ray, 1996). There is also evidence that the population is growing by at least 15% per year (Ray, 1996).

Concerns of Education Professionals

The growth in popularity of home education is seen as innocuous by some and as a positive trend by other observers. On the other hand, however, it is a phenomenon that concerns many government officials, professional educators, and some commonplace citizens. Home education is different from conventional schooling. Reducing the level of control over children on the part of the government, it takes children out of the hands of formally-trained, government-certified teachers, and it places children into the hands of their parents who are not necessarily government certified or professionally trained teachers. Various groups oppose home education. Common and MacMullen (1986, p. 7) asserted:

> The [home education] innovation is resisted because it really threatens many of the assumptions (myths?) that are held to be true in education, such as children learn as a result of the teaching act, children can be best educated in schools, teaching is a highly specialized and complex activity that can best be conducted by trained and licensed people.

Audain (1987, p. 21) characterized professional educators' thoughts another way: "Most conventional educators are leery of the trend to home education. They see an erosion of their job security and power. Some actively try to discourage parents from this option." There are many examples of professional groups discouraging or attempting to tightly control home education (e.g., the National Association of State Boards of Education [NASBE], see references below; the National Education Association [NEA], see references below; and the Parent-Teachers Association, see Lines, 1996, p. 65). For example, the NEA states (Eagle Forum, 1996, p. 4; NEA, 1990, p. 23-24):

> The National Education Association believes that home schooling programs cannot provide the student with a comprehensive education experience. The Association believes that if parental preference home schooling study occurs, students enrolled must meet all state requirements. Instruction should be by persons who are licensed by the appropriate state education licensure agency, and a curriculum approved by the state department of education should be used. The Association further believes that such home schooling programs should be limited to the children of the immediate family, with all expenses being borne by the parents.

The National Association of State Boards of Education (NASBE) (1993, p. 1-2) states:

> . . . decision makers should insure that policies have the following components:
> Strictly enforced registration of home schooled children with the school district . . . Specific provisions for insuring the competency of the instructor . . . . . Assurance that policies with regards to home schooling are aligned with the state's current outcome-based standards and graduation requirements . . . . . Provisions for identifying child abuse in the home.

Further, the National Association of Elementary School Principals (1989-1990, p. 4) ". . . urges local and state associations to support legislation which . . . prohibits at-home schooling as a substitute for compulsory school attendance."

On the other hand, some longtime advocates of home schooling take an antithetical position. Dorian, who holds a master's degree in reading and a Ph.D. in rhetoric and public address, and Tyler, founder and president of a statewide home school organization, for example, claim:

Anyone can homeschool. . . . . . Must the statement *anyone can homeschool* be qualified? Probably—but in a much different way than your common sense may dictate. The qualifying ingredient is not educational credentials or socioeconomic standing—the qualifying ingredient is motivation. Anyone who wants to homeschool can. (Dorian & Tyler, 1996, p. 15)

Despite attempts at dissuasion such as those by the NEA and the NASBE, parents continue to make the choice of home education for their children. Before making the choice to home educate their children, however, many parents, along with professional educators and others, ask numerous questions regarding the effect of home education on children.

Research on Learner Outcomes

Researchers have consistently identified positive outcomes of home education on topics as varied as students' academic achievement, children's social and psychological development, and the performance of the home educated as adults. Some of this literature is reviewed in the following sections. The focus of this review, however, will be on academic achievement as the primary outcome since this is a main focus of this study.

Academic Achievement

Observers often worry that commonplace parents, who are not trained teachers, cannot successfully educate their children. Several investigators have examined the academic achievement of the home educated, and some have postulated reasons for the positive findings indicated to date (Ray, 1989, 1992a).

Such studies often involve an analysis of standardized achievement test scores of home educated students, and therefore a word of explanation is important at this point. It should be noted that the national average on such tests is the 50th percentile. For example, if David scores at the 50th percentile in mathematics, that means he did better than 50 percent of the general nationwide population (i.e., the "norm group") of students who took that mathematics test, and 50% of the students performed better than did David. For another example, if Lucinda scores at the 82nd percentile in science, she performed better than 82 percent of the norm group. For more information about percentiles, see Appendix A.

Generally speaking, children who are taught by their parents score at or above national averages on standardized achievement tests. Following are descriptions of several studies that have investigated the academic achievement of home educated students.

Numerous studies have been conducted in the United States. For example, Wartes, a public high school counselor, has studied the *Stanford Achievement Test* scores of hundreds of home educated students, grades K-12, in Washington State for several years (Wartes, 1987, 1988, 1989, 1990b). Wartes has found that home educated students consistently score above the national average in various academic areas (e.g., reading, language, math, science), with the median score about the 67th percentile.

Rakestraw (1987, 1988) sampled from all elementary age home schooled children in the State of Alabama to obtain the *Stanford Achievement Test* scores of 84 children. She found that the students' academic achievement was at grade level or above in almost all subject areas. Furthermore, the home schooled second grade students scored significantly better than the Alabama public schooled students in reading and listening.

A study in the State of California by Delahooke (1986) compared the intelligence and achievement of home school and private school 9-year-olds. She used private school students because she thought home school students would be more comparable to them in terms of background variables than would public school students. She found no significant differences between the two groups in terms of intelligence and achievement test scores (but she did not report the scores with respect to the national norm).

Students in a state-managed form of home education in Alaska have scored significantly higher than conventional school students nationwide on the *California Achievement Test* in math, reading, language, and science (Alaska Department of Education, 1984, 1985, 1986; Falle, 1986). The Centralized Correspondence Study home school students in Alaska also score higher on achievement tests than do their conventional school peers in Alaska (Alaska Department of Education, 1985, 1986; Falle, 1986).

Both the Oregon Department of Education and the Tennessee Department of Education reported that the home educated students (for whom they have scores) in their states are scoring well above average on standardized achievement tests (Oregon [State] Department of Education, 1993, 1996; Tennessee [State] Department of Education, 1988).

The largest nationwide study to date examined, among other things, the achievement of the home educated from families who are members of the Home School Legal Defense Association. Ray (1990) gathered data on about 1,500 families and 4,600 children. He found that these home educated students averaged at or above the 80th percentile on standardized achievement tests in all tested subject areas. Their scores in "basic" subjects such as reading (84th percentile), language (80th percentile), and mathematics (81st percentile) were particularly noteworthy. In addition, Ray found that home educated students did quite well in areas that skeptics often consider to be too difficult for the untrained to teach, or subject areas in which home educators probably would not be interested. For example, these students scored, on average, at the 84th percentile in science and the 83rd percentile in social studies (Ray, 1990).

The preceding findings by Ray (1990) are somewhat different from the achievement test data that the Home School Legal Defense Association (HSLDA) collected from their membership in 1992 (see Ray, 1992b, p. 10). HSLDA collected the scores of

10,750 students, grades kindergarten through 12, and reported the percentile scores in reading, mathematics, and language at the various grade levels. Average scores (categorized by grade level and subject area) ranged from a low of the 56th percentile to a high of the 84th percentile, with a majority of the percentile scores in the 70s. Perhaps the volunteer nature of participation in Ray's study resulted in the sampling of students whose achievement scores were slightly higher than those in the students sampled by the HSLDA. Other explanations, that will not be discussed here, for the differences are also plausible.

Numerous other studies have yielded findings similar to those just mentioned: home education students in the State of Montana averaged at the 72nd percentile (Ray, 1990a) and at the 73rd percentile (Ray, 1995); the home educated in the State of Pennsylvania scored from the 60th to 74th percentiles (Richman, Girten, & Snyder, 1990); North Dakota students taught at home had averages at about the 85th percentile (Ray, 1991); those taught by their parents in Oklahoma scored, on average, at the 88th percentile in the combination of their reading, language, and mathematics performance (Ray, 1992a).

A Canada nationwide study examined 2,594 children in 808 families (Ray, 1994). These children, taught at home by their parents, performed similarly to their United States counterparts in terms of academic achievement. Their scores, on average, were at the 80th percentile in reading, 84th percentile in listening, 76th percentile in language, 76th percentile in language, 79th percentile in math, 82nd percentile in science, and the 81st percentile in social studies. Another study in Canada (Priesnitz & Priesnitz, 1990) revealed that 32% of the children tested were above average in their scores, 4% were below average, and apparently the other 64% were average (but the report did not specify this).

Not all studies, however, show home educated students scoring above average. Rakestraw (1987, 1988) found 1st and 4th grade home education students to be scoring below the national average in mathematics, while the home educated in grades 2, 3, 5, and 6 were above average in math. These students, on the other hand, were above average in their reading for the 1st through 6th grades with scores at the 54th through 97th percentiles. The

Washington State Superintendent of Public Instruction (WSSPI) (1985) also found scores that were not particularly high. The WSSPI reported the home educated scoring at the 62nd percentile in reading, 53rd percentile in mathematics, and the 56th percentile in language—modestly above average.

Correlations Between Academic Achievement and Other Variables

A number of researchers have explored whether the academic achievement of the home educated is related to selected variables that might be of particular interest to policy makers. One of the factors of interest is whether the parents are state-certified (i.e., government-certified) teachers. Rakestraw (1988) explored the relationship in Alabama; Havens (1991) studied the home educated in Texas; and Ray (1990b) did the same nationwide in the United States, nationwide in Canada (Ray, 1994), and specifically in Oklahoma (Ray, 1992a). In all of these studies there was no statistically significant relationship between students' achievement and the teacher certification status of their parents.

The formal educational attainment of parents is another factor that is of interest to policy makers and researchers. Havens (1991), Rakestraw (1988), and Ray (1992a) all found no relationship between parents' educational attainment and the academic achievement scores of their home-educated children in Texas, Alabama, and Oklahoma. On the other hand, Ray found weak to moderate relationships between parents' educational attainment and their children's achievement scores in his nationwide (Ray, 1990b), North Dakota (Ray, 1991), and Canada (Ray, 1994) studies. Likewise, Wartes (1990a) found weak to moderate relationships in his Washington research. Even with these correlations, which do not necessarily indicate a causal relationship, the home educated children of parents with lower formal educational attainment still tended to score above average on achievement tests.

Finally, the relationship between family income and student achievement has been of interest to policy makers and researchers. "Within the general school population, . . . The children of parents who earn more money tend to do better than those where the parents earn less" (Wartes, 1990a, p. 50). There was no significant relationship between family income and student achievement in home school studies done in North Dakota (Ray, 1991), in most comparisons in an Oklahoma study (Ray, 1992a), and in Canada (Ray, 1994). On the other hand, Wartes (1990a) and Ray (Ray, 1990b) found weak relationships between income and test scores in Washington and in a nationwide study. Even with these weak correlations, which do not necessarily indicate causal relationship, the home educated generally scored above average.

Research to date, which has been largely descriptive in nature, indicates that the academic achievement of the home educated is typically above average compared to that of students in public schools. Most of the studies on the academic achievement of the home educated have been limited to one or a few states in their scope. Only one significant study has been nationwide, and that was done over five years ago. Very little of the research has been longitudinal and, therefore, little is known about how the children's achievement or the families' characteristics change over time. Addressing some of these limitations, this study also will include a nationwide sample of families and their children and it will explore the changes over time of families and children who were included in an earlier nationwide study (Ray, 1990b).

Social and Psychological Characteristics

There is a smaller body of research that deals with the social and psychological development of home educated children and the social lives of home school families. First, the weight of evidence to date is that the self-concept (and self-esteem) of home educated students is comparable to, and usually stronger than, that of children in conventional schools (Hedin, 1991; Kelly, 1991; Medlin, 1994; Shyers, 1992; Taylor, 1986; Tillman, 1995). Home educated students have been found to be as adept or more adept than conventional school students in the areas of social interaction and social skills (Carson, 1990; Chatham-Carpenter, 1994; Delahooke, 1986; Johnson, 1991; Shyers, 1992; Smedley, 1992). Findings to date show that home educated children regularly participate in social activities such as youth programs, sports, church or synagogue school, classes with other children, and volunteer activities (Ray, 1992a, 1994, 1995; Wartes, 1987). A few studies have been done on youth and adults who were home educated. They are active in extracurricular activities in a way that would prepare them for leadership in adulthood (Montgomery, 1989); they perform well in college English courses (Galloway & Sutton, 1995); those in college possess thinking skills that are comparable to those who were taught in conventional schools (Oliveira, Watson, & Sutton, 1994); and home educated adults are employed, independent-minded, and entrepreneurial adults who think positively about their home-education experiences (Knowles & Muchmore, 1995).

2

Methodology

This study included cross-sectional descriptive, multivariate, and longitudinal design elements. Various aspects of the plan and execution of the study are described in this chapter.

The Instrument

The instrument (Appendix B) for this study was based on the surveys (questionnaires) designed and successfully used by Ray (1990b, 1994). It also contained selected items from the National Assessment of Educational Progress (NAEP) (United States Department of Education, Office of Educational Research and Improvement, 1992) and the National Education Longitudinal Survey (NELS) (United States Department of Education, Office of Educational Research and Improvement, 1996a). Current literature on home education and the objectives of this study were also considered in the development of the survey.

The Ray (1990b, 1994) instruments were designed by a cooperative effort of the researcher and others who had expertise in home education in the United States. The guidelines for conducting survey research delineated by Borg and Gall (1989) were followed for Ray's studies and for the present study. The present instrument was designed to answer the research questions for this study (and research questions for other studies related to home education that may be pursued at a later date). This instrument was reviewed and revised by persons who are familiar with home education (e.g., home school leaders and researchers) and consensus was reached on the validity of the items and their wording.

The instrument has four parts:
- A. Descriptive information regarding parents and family (e.g., demographics, teacher certification status of parents).
- B. Information regarding the home education legal status of the family (e.g., contact with public school officials and with attorneys).
- C. Information regarding the students (e.g., demographics, years home schooled, academic achievement scores, curriculum used).
- D. Information regarding volunteering to participate in a longitudinal study (e.g., parents' names, address).

Parts A, B, and D consisted of five pages of items and Part C consisted of four pages of items per child in the family. The majority of items were select-type (or forced-choice) format and involved the respondent simply marking one of two or more categories. A small portion of the items were open-ended and required respondents to supply written responses. Where appropriate, space was given for the respondents to write out "other" responses that did not fit the given categories.

The instrument resulted in 190 variables being available for analysis: 99 per family and 91 per child. Recoding and the creation of additional variables for analysis was done later.

Definitions

Several terms used in this study are defined in this section.

Academic Achievement - Formal demonstration of learning (including knowledge, understanding, and thinking skills) attained by a student as measured by standardized academic achievement tests. For example, knowledge and ability in the areas of reading, language, and mathematics are included.

Degree of Structure - The degree of structure in the practice of home education varies greatly. It ranges from a very unstructured (unschooling) learning approach, centered upon the child's interests, to the use of a planned, structured, and highly prescribed curriculum. Given the preceding explanation, parents rated their own practice on a 7-point scale from "very unstructured" (with a value of 1) to very structured (with a value of 7).

Formal Instruction - Formal instruction is planned or intentional instruction in areas such as reading, writing, spelling, or arithmetic. It is done to meet a learning objective.

Structured Learning Time - Structured learning is time during which the child is engaged in learning activities planned by the parent; it is a time during which the child is not free to do whatever he or she chooses.

Population and Sample

The target population was all families in the United States who were educating their school-age children at home. An attempt was made to utilize a sample that was more representative than the one studied by Ray (1990b). Ray's sample was drawn only from the membership of one large nationwide home education organization. In the present study, home education families from this same membership organization and from many other organizations and other lists were asked to participate.

Linear systematic sampling was used to select families from the lists of various national and statewide organizations. Linear systematic sampling closely approximates random sampling (Borg & Gall, 1989, p. 224; Fowler, 1988, p. 23-24, 39).

Religious affiliation is one of the major factors that discriminates among home educators in many respects (Hood, 1991; Ray, 1993; Van Galen, 1988). Whereas Ray (1990b) found that 94% of fathers and 96% of mothers described themselves as "born-again Christians," other researchers have made different findings. For example, percentages that represent this category of basic biblical Christians have included 78% (Mayberry, 1988), 97% (Wartes, 1990a), 87% (Ray, 1995), 40% (and an additional 24% were Mormon/Latter-Day Saints; Knowles, Mayberry, & Ray, 1991), 34% (Gustafson, 1987; nationwide, sampling through a secular organization), and 94% (Ray, 1992a).

This present study attempted to include a more representative sampling of home educators, with respect to religion, than did Ray's 1990 nationwide study. Based on previously cited literature and data from organizations and periodicals that serve home educators, the researcher inferred that approximately 83% of home educators identify themselves as Christians. Therefore, a purposeful attempt was made to locate and include in the sample about 17% who would not identify themselves as born-again or basic biblical Christians.

Home education support organizations, and contacts via word-of-mouth and personal networks, assisted in contacting home education families throughout the country. One well-known national organization, in particular, played a prominent role in distributing the survey instrument throughout the country via direct mail, articles in home education publications, and telephone contacts. Surveys were also mailed to all families who participated in Ray's (1990b) study who could be located. (One reason for cooperating with this organization was that it was involved in the 1990 study by Ray and could help identify and contact families involved in that study.) This combination of using support organizations, publications, and word-of-mouth was the best way of contacting the widest variety of home educators in a practical and efficient manner. This method of utilizing support organizations for making contact with a variety of home education families has been successfully used in prior research (e.g., Knowles, Mayberry, & Ray, 1991; Ray, 1990b, 1991, 1992a, 1994; Richman, Girten, & Snyder, 1990). One of the reasons for the success of this approach is that home educators often trust other home educators and their organizations more than they trust government agencies or researchers. This is not to say, however, that this method (or any other reasonable method) would either (1) necessarily result in a representative sample of home education families or (2) necessarily introduce sampling bias.

Pilot Study

No pilot study was done in the present study for the following reasons: (a) a pilot study was done in Ray's (1990b, 1994) nationwide United States and Canada studies which were very similar to this study, (b) similar instruments and research designs had been used by the researcher in several previous studies on home education (Ray, 1990b, 1994, 1995), and (c) there was no reason to predict that this study would pose significant differences in terms of how home educators would respond to this instrument and study.

Distribution and Collection of the Instrument, and Response Rate

First class mail was used to distribute a total of 5,995 copies of the instrument to individual home education families and home education support groups in all states from late January to late February 1996. A letter of transmittal was included with each copy. Multiple copies (either 10 or 15, depending on the nature of the support organization) were sent to individual support groups for further distribution to individual families (i.e., a total of 3,450 surveys to be distributed by organizations). Support group leaders were given instructions about how to select a representative sample of potential participants. Two hundred forty-nine surveys were returned with no marks on them and apparently not delivered to home education families; the researcher assumed that these never reached individual families. The researcher estimated that instruments reached up to a *maximum* of 5,746 individual homes via mailing lists and support group leaders. Follow-up reminders (either letters in envelopes or postcards) were sent via first class mail to all individual families and support organizations in mid-March 1996.

All usable instruments returned were included in this study. The total number of completed and usable instruments included in the study was 1,657 (i.e., 1,657 families, including information on 5,200 children), which is equivalent to a response rate of 28.8% *or more*.

It is possible that a large percentage of the support organizations did not forward the surveys to individual families, especially since some home school organizations and leaders are antagonistic toward research efforts (e.g., Kaseman & Kaseman, 1991; Mayberry, Knowles, Ray, & Marlow, 1995, p. 4-5). If half of the surveys sent to organizations were not distributed to individual families, then only 4,021 reached families and the response rate was 41%. There was no practical way to validate how many surveys reached individual families.

The minimum response rate of 28.8% compares favorably with that of 24.7% reported by Knowles, Mayberry, and Ray (1991) who dealt with a wide variety of home education organizations and a variety of means of obtaining names and addresses of home educators. This minimum response rate of 28.8% is also comparable to the 31.3% response rate reported by Ray (1994). A possible higher response rate (of, e.g., 41%) would be even more favorable. The response rate for this study is typical of what can be expected in this type of social science research (Fowler, 1988). On the other hand, the response rate in this study is considerably lower than the 70.1% reported by Ray (1990b), who was working solely with the membership of one organization that strongly motivated its member families to participate.

After the data for the families that were involved in Ray's 1990 study (n = 275) were merged with the same families involved in this study, there were data available on 5,402 children in the 1,657 families. Analyses for (1) this study's 1,657 families and their 5,200 children, (2) comparative data involving this study's data and the 1990 study, and (3) the families that participated in both the1990 study and this study were kept separate.

Since it was not known who did not respond, an analysis of non-respondents could not be done. No adjustments in the data analyses were made with respect to non-response.

Data Entry, Data Analysis, and Statistical Hypotheses

Data entry was done by hand utilizing *Microsoft Excel (Version 5.0)* (Microsoft Corporation, 1994) and *SPSS for Windows (Version 6.1.2)* (SPSS, Inc., 1995). *SPSS for Windows* was used for data analysis.

Students' scores on tests were handled in the following manner. The questionnaire asked for students' national percentile ranks on various test components and batteries. Parents usually reported percentiles as requested and typically attached photocopies (as requested by the researcher) of their students' scores as provided by a testing service. When copies were provided, the reported percentiles were checked and corrected when appropriate. Very few errors were detected. In addition, linear systematic sampling was used to select 5% of the families for a verification of the accuracy of data entry; data entry was sufficiently accurate. Percentiles were converted to z-scores (Hopkins, Glass, & Hopkins, 1987, Appendix Table A; see also the Appendix in this report). Means were calculated and statistical tests were performed using z-scores. For this study, z-scores were used because they provided the most reasonable way to aggregate scores from many students using a variety of tests, and to analyze how those scores compared to standardized test norms and to each other. It is not assumed in this study that scores on different tests mean, necessarily, the same thing about the students who took them (Gronlund & Linn, 1990), nor is it assumed that students in this study are perfectly analogous to those students represented by norms for the standardized tests that these students took. It is assumed, however, that the use of aggregated scores from a variety of standardized achievement tests is an acceptable practice and provides valuable information (Frisbie, 1992; Hunter & Schmidt, 1990, p. 516-518).

In many cases, simple descriptive statistics and frequencies were appropriate and reported. A number of hypotheses related to the research questions were tested. The hypothesis tested in all cases was the null hypothesis. For example, in testing correlations, the hypothesis was that there was no relationship between the variables. In comparing groups, the hypothesis was that there was no difference between the groups.

Alpha was set at 0.01 for statistical tests in this study. Alpha is the ". . . level of significance used to decide whether to accept or reject a [statistical] null hypothesis..." (Borg & Gall, 1989, p. 352). Alpha was set at 0.01 for several reasons. First, this level of alpha (rather than .05 or .10, for example) helps to take into account multiple error rate (Good, 1984). Second, this approach was consistent with prior research (Ray, 1990b, 1994). Finally, this level of alpha helps reduce the probability of *Type I error* in this situation where the rejection of a true null hypothesis might involve potential harm to people like those involved in the study (Shavelson, 1988, p. 286). For example, concluding that there is a statistically significant (or practically significant) relationship between parents' teacher certification status and children's academic achievement, when in fact there is none, could do serious harm to family integrity and children's learning in terms of subsequent policy decisions related to home education.

The study was designed to provide basic demographic statistics and other data regarding the home education families and their children. In addition, the following hypotheses were to be tested; some of these were stated and used as statistical null hypotheses:

Hypothesis 1. There is no significant relationship between the dependent variable of student academic achievement and the following independent variables:

    (a) highest formal education level attained by the father;

    (b) highest formal education level attained by the mother;

    (c) teacher certification status of the father (i.e., whether the father had ever been a certified teacher);

    (d) teacher certification status of the mother (i.e., whether the mother had ever been a certified teacher);

    (e) family income;

    (f) amount of money spent on the home education of the student;

    (g) legal status of the family (Table 3);

    (h) gender of the student;

    (i) the number of years the student was home educated;

    (j) the extent to which the family visits public libraries;

    (k) the time spent in formal educational activities;

    (l) the age at which formal education of the student commenced;

    (m) the degree of regulation of home education by the state;

    (n) who administered the achievement test; and

    (o) the use of a computer in the education of the student.

Independent variables (a) through (l) were addressed using multiple regression; (m) through (o) were addressed via tests of comparison.

Hypothesis 2. There is no significant difference over time (about 6 years) in the following for students who were involved in both Ray's 1990 study and in this study:

    (a) achievement test scores, and

    (b) kind of curriculum used.

Hypothesis 3. There is no significant difference in basic demographics and other characteristics regarding families and children involved in Ray's 1990 study compared to those involved in this study.

Hypothesis 4. There is no significant difference in the following for the families who were involved in both Ray's 1990 study and in this study:
  (a) father's education level;
  (b) mother's education level;
  (c) family income;
  (f) number of years child was home educated;
  (g) number of visits to public libraries; and
  (h) amount of money spent per child per year for home education.

Assumptions

The researcher assumed that parents and their children (their students) were honest and accurate in completing the self-report surveys. It was assumed that parents and their students were the ones who would have the most accurate information, for the purposes of this study, about the functioning of home education for their family. The researcher also assumed that only one survey per family was completed.

Finally, the author assumed that the standardized achievement tests, from which scores were reported in this study, are reasonably reliable and valid and that they were properly administered and scored. There is a large literature base on the standardized achievement tests that is mentioned in this study that is accessible to those interested in exploring the validity and reliability of those instruments (e.g., Mitchell, 1983, 1985). In general, these tests have very high validity and reliability coefficients of about .90 (Borg & Gall, 1989; Hopkins & Stanley, 1981).

Delimitations and Limitations

Although this study addresses numerous objectives, it is important to recognize significant delimitations and limitations.

Delimitations

This study does not examine the extent to which several objectives of home education parents are met (Cizek, 1991, 1993; Ray, 1988). For example, there is no focused assessment of whether the children develop psychologically, emotionally, and socially according to their parents' plans and desires, whether children adhere more or less to their parents' belief system than do children in public or private conventional schools, nor whether these children make better adult citizens than do those who never experienced home education.

This is not a causal-comparative study (Borg & Gall, 1989). That is, background variables in this *ex post facto* study are not controlled in such a way as to make possible conclusions about the causes of academic achievement test scores being higher (or lower) than those of students in conventional schools. This study is not designed to determine whether type of schooling (i.e., home versus public or conventional) causes differential academic achievement. The findings, however, may ultimately suggest causality.

Limitations

First, the sample in this study is composed of volunteers and therefore characteristics of volunteers must be considered when interpreting the findings. For example, volunteers tend to be better educated and have higher social-class status than nonvolunteers (Borg & Gall, 1989, p. 228).

Second, it is practically impossible to include a random sample of all home education families in the United States or the complete population for a study such as this. The "population and sample" section above addresses this issue. It is important, therefore, to keep in mind the limitations of representativeness and generalizability.

Third, this study is descriptive and exploratory in nature. It is one of the relatively few nationwide studies that have been completed on home education. It is apparently the first study that has been made public which is of such large magnitude and includes a longitudinal component, and it provides detailed descriptive and comparative statistical analyses. Despite these characteristics, however, many questions are yet to be answered about home education in the United States.

3

Findings

This findings section will present, in the form of descriptive statistics and the results of statistical analyses, the data that were collected. A later section will summarize the findings and make comparisons between them and comparable data for families in America in general and to students in conventional schools. The latter section will also include interpretation of the data.

Family Characteristics

Several findings were made relating to the 1,657 families and 5,402 children involved in this study. Some of these findings are presented in this section; others are presented elsewhere in this report.

Basic demographics

Tables 1 through 6 and Figures 1 through 9 present some of the summary statistics on home education families in this study; a limited number of these details are emphasized in this section.

The average formal education of the father was 15.6 years, or about 3 years of college; the average was 14.7 years for the mother (Figures 1 and 2). About 32% of the parents had earned a bachelor's degree. Fifty-three percent of the families visited public libraries 1 to 2 times per month, 32% did so 3 to 4 times per month, and 15% visited public libraries 5 or more times per month (Figure 9). The average number of visits per month to any kind of library was 3.8.

(Please note that most of the tables and figures in this report contain more information than is reported in the body of the text of this report. The body of the text usually includes summaries and data that represent categories containing the majority of cases.)

In terms of occupation, 17% of the fathers classified themselves as a professional such as an accountant, registered nurse, engineer, banker, or librarian, and 17% were professionals such as a minister, dentist, doctor, lawyer, or college teacher, and 11% of the fathers were small business owners (see Figure 3). (Two professional categories were used in order to be consistent with methodology used by the federal government; cf., United States Department of Education, National Center for Education Statistics, 1992). Eighty-eight percent of the mothers were in the homemaker/home educator category; 4.8% were professionals such as accountants, registered nurses, engineers, bankers, or librarians (see Figure 4). Sixteen percent of the mothers worked outside the home; those who did worked an average of 14 hours per week outside the home. The median annual family income was $43,000; 25% of the families were in the category of $35,000 through $49,999 per year and 27% had an annual income of $50,000 through $74,999 (Figure 5).

Mothers did 88% of the formal instruction of their children, fathers did about 10% of the formal instruction, and other people (e.g., a family member, a tutor) did about 3% of the formal instruction of the students.

Ninety-six percent of the fathers and 96% of the mothers were white (not Hispanic) in terms of race/ethnicity (Figures 6 and 7). About 1.5% of the parents were Hispanic and 1% were Asian, Pacific Islander, or Oriental. All of the other categories listed in the survey were also represented.

The average number of children per family was 3.3. Thirty-eight percent of the families had 4 or more children. Ninety-eight percent of the families for whom data were available were headed by married couples. (Data were missing for 28 of 1,650 families.) Only 2% of the respondents (26 of 1,286 families) were single parents, and 17 of 20 (data were unavailable for 6) of these were mothers.

The respondents reported that they spend, on average, $546 per child per year for home education; the median was $400. Respondents were asked to include, for example, tuition, textbooks, field trips, and special resources in their estimate. Dollar amounts for this item ranged from 0.2% of the families reporting $0, to 13% reporting $500 (the mode), to 6% reporting $600, to 0.01% (one family) reporting $20,000.

Eighty-six percent of the families have a computer in their home (Table 1). Computers are used for the education of children in 84% of these families.

The states and territories in which the families lived are presented in Table 2. All 50 states, the District of Columbia, Guam, Puerto Rico, and the Virgin Islands were represented. The seven states that each comprised at least 3% of the sample were Texas (6.5%), California (6.3%), Virginia (4.8%), Washington (4.6%), Ohio (4.2%), New York (3.6%), and Pennsylvania (3%). Table 2 also presents, for comparative purposes, the percent of the general United States population that resides in each state and territory.

Table 3 presents the families' legal status with respect to home education law. Of the 1,479 respondents, 78% had satisfied statutory requirements and 6% classified themselves as "underground." Underground generally means that the parents had not notified government authorities that they home educate their children, or the parents were trying to avoid the government having knowledge of their practice of home education. Parents often chose "other" ($N = 196$) when they could not easily classify themselves in one of the categories provided on the questionnaire.

Of the 1,458 families who responded to the item asking whether they had submitted any paperwork to state or local school authorities to notify them of their home schooling, 62.4% said "yes" and 37.6% answered "no."

Variable	Mean	Standard Deviation	Sample Size
Father's Years of Formal Education	15.61	2.92	1602
Mother's Years of Formal Education	14.66	2.14	1625
Age of Children Currently Home Educated	10.48	3.43	3568
Number of Children per Family	3.33	1.57	1624
Percent of Income Earned by Father	94.69	15.55	1594
Percent of Income Earned by Mother	4.91	14.45	1582
Mothers Who Work Outside the Home — 16.2%			
Hours/Week They Work Outside Home	13.99	10.80	262
Cost ($) per Child per Year to			
Home Educate	546.33	724.52	1558
Median Family Income — $43,000 *	52,459	45.909	1522
Visits to Public Library per Month	3.00	2.25	1499
Visits to Any Library per Month	3.79	3.57	1557
Computer in Home of Family — 85.6%			
Computer Used for Education — 83.7%			
Get A Newspaper Regularly — 68.6%			
Get Magazines Regularly — 96.3%			
Associate With A Home School Organization — 95.4%			
Subscribe To A Home Education Publication — 78.2%			
Formal Teaching—Percent by Father	9.72	12.24	1541
Formal Teaching—Percent by Mother	87.81	16.62	1611
Formal Teaching—Percent by Other Adult	3.37	12.91	1379
Fathers Who Have Ever Been Certified to Teach— 6.5% (of those responding)			
Mothers Who Have Ever Been Certified to Teach — 15.4% (of those responding)			

* Median income is the figure most commonly reported in research and government reports.

Table 1. General characteristics of the home educating families.

Teacher certification

Six percent of the fathers had been or were currently certified teachers; 15% of the mothers had been or were currently certified teachers (Table 1).

Religious affiliation

In terms of religious preference of the fathers, 23% were independent fundamental/evangelical (Christian), 19% were Baptist, 9% were independent charismatic (Christian), 5% were Roman Catholic, 1% were atheist, and 0.3% were Jewish. Religious preference of the mothers was similar: 23% were independent fundamental/evangelical (Christian), 19% were Baptist, 9% were independent charismatic (Christian), 5% were Roman Catholic, 0.5% were atheist, and 0.3% were Jewish (Tables 4 and 5). Eleven percent to 12% selected "Other" for their religious affiliation.

The religious affiliation of 186 fathers and 182 mothers (11% to 12% of parents) who chose "other" for their religious affiliation was examined. About 56% of the religions listed would be classified, by the author, as biblically-based Christian; most of these would fall into the category of evangelical, fundamental, or conservative mainline Christian. Other common self-descriptors were "none" (about 7%), Unitarian Universalist (about 6%), New Age-related (about 5%), agnostic (about 4%), and a few individuals each responded pagan, Zen Buddhist, pantheistic, or religious science.

For those families who responded to the items regarding being "born again" Christians, 83% of the fathers were "born again" and 86% of the mothers were likewise.

As explained in the methodology section, the researcher inferred that approximately 83% of home educators identify themselves as Christian and that a purposeful attempt was made to locate and include in the sample about 17% who would not identify themselves as Christian. It appears that about 84% to 90% of the parents involved in this study would identify themselves as biblically-based Christians. Therefore, the percentage who were non-Christians was perhaps lower than what was targeted.

State	Freq.	%	U.S. % [1]
AK	18	1.2	0.22
AL	8	.5	1.62
AR	13	.9	0.95
AZ	13	.9	1.47
CA	94	6.3	11.97
CO	22	1.5	1.32
CT	17	1.1	1.32
DC	2	.1	0.24
DE	19	1.3	0.27
FL	44	2.9	5.20
GA	33	2.2	2.60
GU	10	.7	see note
HI	7	.5	0.45
IA	19	1.3	1.12
ID	18	1.2	0.40
IL	36	2.4	4.60
IN	21	1.4	2.23
KS	30	2.0	1.00
KY	30	2.0	1.48
LA	12	.8	1.70
MA	14	.9	2.42
MD	37	2.5	1.92
ME	17	1.1	0.49
MI	35	2.3	3.74
MN	31	2.1	1.76
MO	23	1.5	2.06
MS	19	1.3	1.03
MT	23	1.5	0.32
NC	19	1.3	2.67
ND	7	.5	0.26
NE	27	1.8	0.63
NH	17	1.1	0.45
NJ	16	1.1	3.11
NM	31	2.1	0.61
NV	6	.4	0.48
NY	54	3.6	7.23
OH	63	4.2	4.36
OK	30	2.0	1.26
OR	20	1.3	1.14
PA	45	3.0	4.78
PR	1	.1	see note
RI	4	.3	0.40
SC	20	1.3	1.40
SD	20	1.3	0.28
TN	52	3.5	1.96
TX	97	6.5	6.83
UT	22	1.5	0.69
VA	72	4.8	2.49
VI	2	.1	see note
VT	19	1.3	0.23
WA	68	4.6	1.96
WI	44	2.9	1.97
WV	32	2.1	0.72
WY	40	2.7	0.18
Total	1493	99.8	100

Note 1. 1990 United States census; territories not included in 100% total (Famighetti, 1995).

Table 2. States and territories of residence of home education families.

Category	Frequency	Percent
Underground	83	5.6
Notified District, Not Attempting to Fully Comply	37	2.5
Satisfied Statutes	1161	78.5
Legal Status in Dispute	2	.1
Other	196	13.3
Total	1479	100.0

Table 3. Legal status of the families with respect to home education statutes.

Grandparents' support of home education

Table 6 provides information about the responses of the children's grandparents to the family's practice of home education. Responses included "opposed," "opposed, but not interfering," "neutral," "originally opposed, now supportive," "supportive," and "supportive and participating." Fifty-nine percent of the paternal grandparents supported the home education, while 74% of the maternal grandparents supported it. Twenty-eight percent of the paternal grandparents and 17% of the maternal grandparents were neutral toward their children home educating their grandchildren. Thirteen percent of the paternal and 9% of the maternal grandparents were opposed to the home schooling.

Religion	Freq.	%
Adventist (Seventh-day)	7	.4
Assembly of God	75	4.7
Baptist	299	18.6
Episcopal	10	.6
Independent Charismatic	136	8.5
Independent Fundamental/ Evangelical	365	22.7
Lutheran	26	1.6
Mennonite	14	.9
Methodist	29	1.8
Nazarene	12	.7
Pentecostal	43	2.7
Presbyterian	56	3.5
Reformed	58	3.6
Other Protestant	54	3.4
Catholic (Roman)	83	5.2
Eastern Orthodox	2	.1
Other Christian	90	5.6
LDS (Latter-Day Saint)	19	1.2
Jehovah's Witness	5	.3
Jewish	5	.3
Muslim	1	.1
Buddhist	5	.3
New Age	9	.6
Other Eastern Religion	3	.2
Atheist	14	.9
Other	186	11.6

Total   1606

Table 4. Fathers' religious affiliation.

Religion	Freq.	%
Adventist (Seventh-day)	8	.5
Assembly of God	76	4.7
Baptist	305	18.9
Episcopal	11	.7
Independent Charismatic	144	8.9
Independent Fundamental/ Evangelical	373	23.1
Lutheran	23	1.4
Mennonite	16	1.0
Methodist	26	1.6
Nazarene	13	.8
Pentecostal	46	2.8
Presbyterian	61	3.8
Reformed	54	3.3
Other Protestant	51	3.2
Catholic (Roman)	83	5.1
Eastern Orthodox	3	.2
Other Christian	87	5.4
LDS (Latter-Day Saint)	19	1.2
Jehovah's Witness	7	.4
Jewish	5	.3
Muslim	1	.1
Buddhist	2	.1
New Age	10	.6
Other Eastern Religion	2	.1
Atheist	8	.5
Other	182	11.3

Total   1616

Table 5. Mothers' religious affiliation.

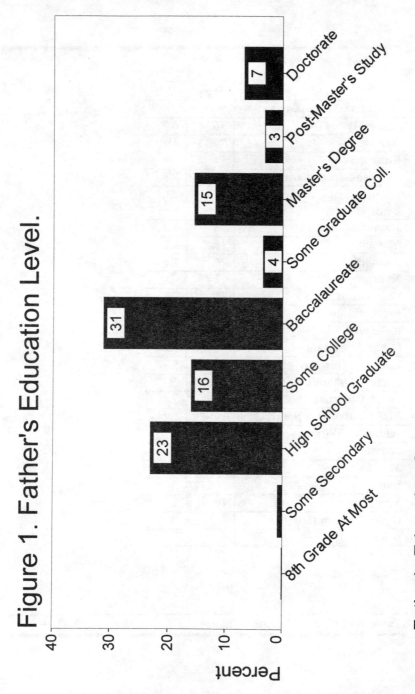

Figure 1. Father's Education Level.

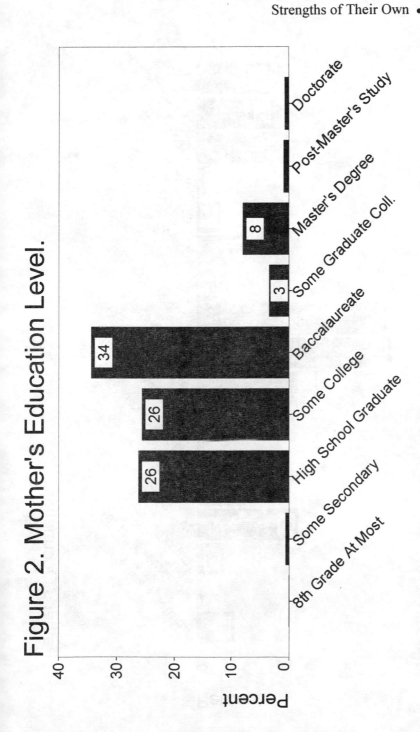

Figure 2. Mother's Education Level.

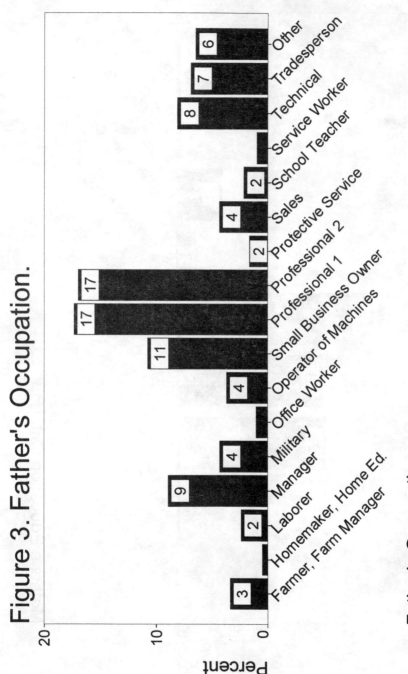

Figure 3. Father's Occupation.

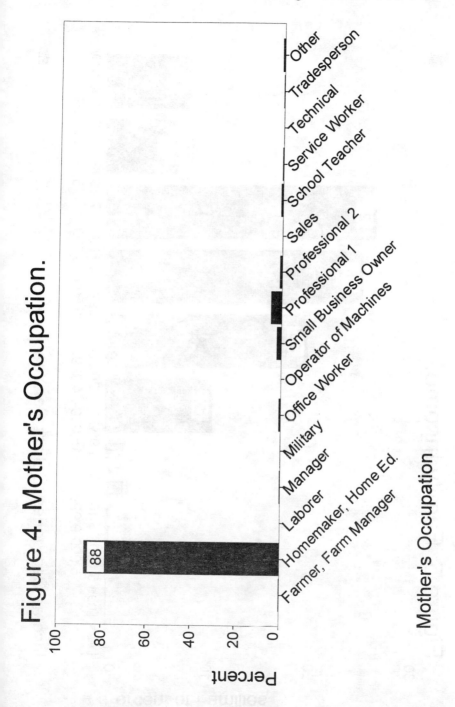

Figure 4. Mother's Occupation.

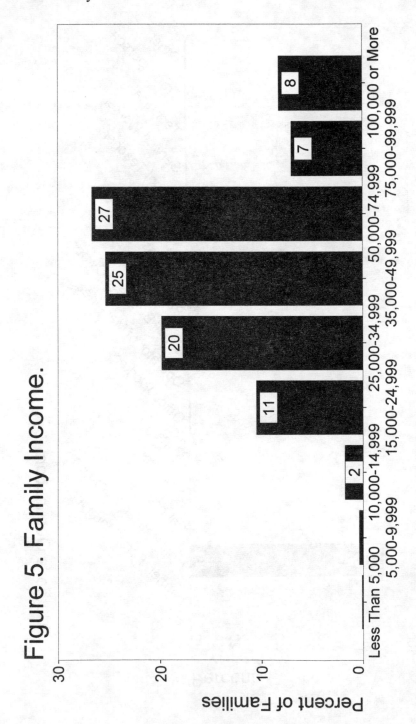

Figure 5. Family Income.

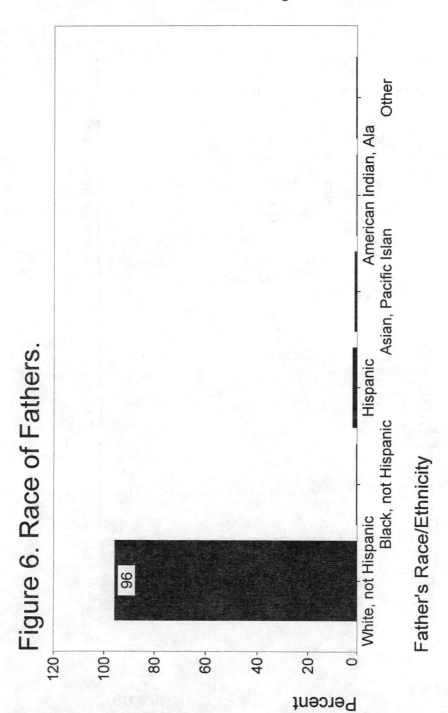

Figure 6. Race of Fathers.

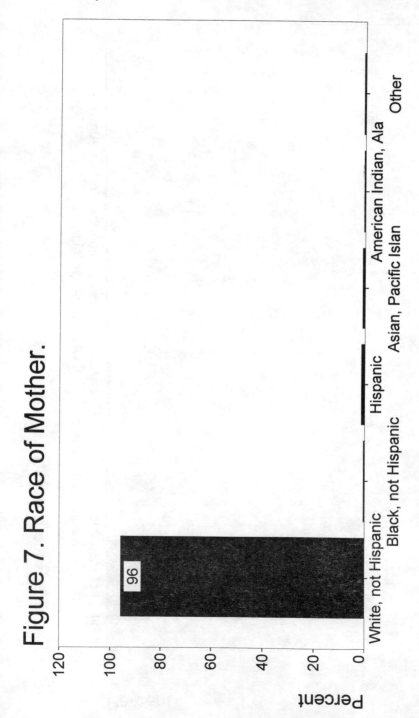

Figure 7. Race of Mother.

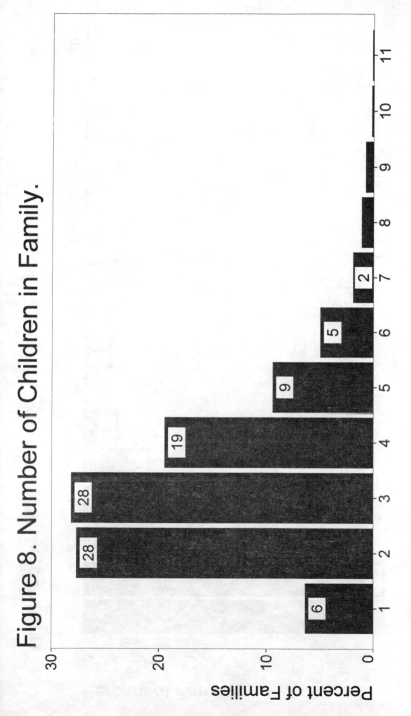

Figure 8. Number of Children in Family.

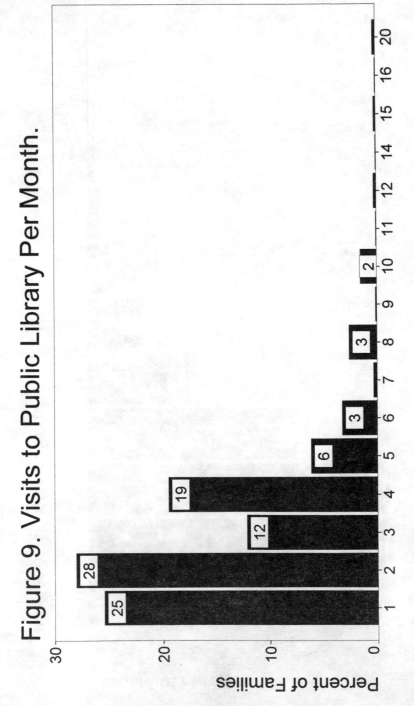

Figure 9. Visits to Public Library Per Month.

Children's Characteristics

Tables 7 through 13 and Figures 10 and 11 present several pieces of information about the children in these families. The average number of children in the family was 3.3 (median = 3, mode = 3); 27.6% of the families had 2 children, 28.1% had 3, and 19.5% had 4. The average age of the children who were being home educated in the families was 10.5 years (median = 10, mode = 8) (Table 7). The average grade level of the students who were being home educated was 4.8. Grades 1 through 8 included 77% while grades 9 through 12 included 14% of the students (Table 11). Only 15 school-age children in these families had never been home educated.

When parents were asked through which grade they intended to home educate their currently home educated children, they said they would home educate 5% of the children through the 8th grade, 76% through the 12th grade, and 10% through college (Figure 10). Of the children being home educated, 50.4% were males and 49.6% were females. In terms of the race/ethnic group of the children being home educated (N = 3,569), 94.9% were white (not Hispanic), 0.4% Black (not Hispanic), 1.2% Hispanic, 0.9% were Asian, Pacific Islander, or Oriental, 0.4% American Indian or Alaskan Native, and 2.0% were reported as "Other."

Paternal Grandparents

Response	Freq.	%
Opposed	18	1.2
Opposed, But Not Interfering	181	12.0
Neutral	416	27.6
Originally Opposed, Now Supportive	279	18.5
Supportive	546	36.3
Supportive And Participating	65	4.3

Total   1505

Maternal Grandparents

Response	Freq.	%
Opposed	13	.8
Opposed, But Not Interfering	129	8.3
Neutral	266	17.2
Originally Opposed, Now Supportive	315	20.3
Supportive	653	42.2
Supportive And Participating	173	11.2

Total   1549

Table 6. Response of children's grandparents to the family practicing home education.

Variable	Mean	S.D.	Sample Size
Age	10.48	3.43	3568
Grade	4.81	3.25	3199
Degree Of Structure	4.84	1.54	3570
Hours Structured Learning Per Day	3.61	1.57	3537
Age Formal Instruction Began	5.71	1.70	3491
Contact With Non-family Adults, hours/week	9.66	7.57	3516
Awake With Siblings, hours/week	73.10	27.32	3435
With Non-sibling Children, hours/week	10.90	8.07	3506
Years Home Educated Since Age 5	4.75	2.80	3480
Years Of Public School Prior To Home Schooling	.98	1.89	2248
Years Of Private School Prior To Home Schooling	.62	1.34	2103
Years Of Public School After Home Schooling	.06	.38	1829
Years Of Private School After To Home Schooling	.07	.49	1826
Grade Through Which Intend To Home Educate Child	11.83	2.47	2697

Table 7. General descriptive information about children being home educated.

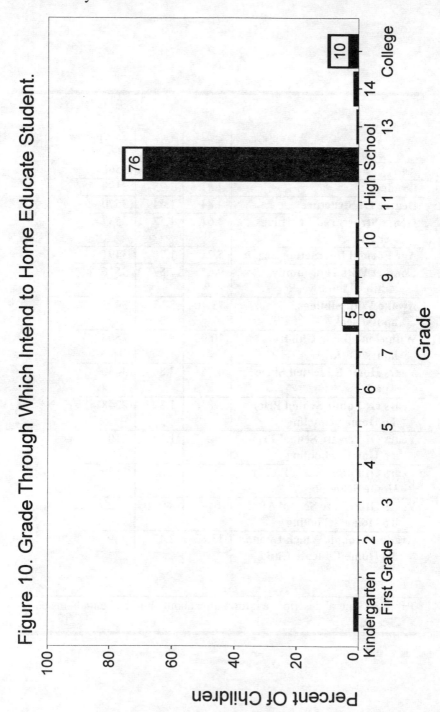

Figure 10. Grade Through Which Intend to Home Educate Student.

Curriculum

Parents were asked about the kind of curriculum materials they used for their children, and they could choose more than one kind per student (i.e., the total selected could exceed 100%). Table 12 shows the results. The parents used a parent-designed curriculum (i.e., the major components were hand-picked or selected by the parents, often from various curriculum suppliers) for 71% of the students, a complete curriculum package (i.e., included language, social studies, mathematics, and science material for a full year) for 24% of the students, no particular curriculum plan for 6% of the students, a local private school's home education program for 1% of the students, and a satellite school (i.e., materials from a private school or educational organization that works with the home educated at a distance) for 3% of the students.

A Beka publishers was the most common complete curriculum package as it was used for 31% of the students in this category (complete curricular package) (Table 13). Bob Jones University Press was used by 16% in this category and Christian Liberty Academy was used by 11%.

Children's activities

Table 8 presents some of the types of social activities in which the currently home educated children were involved. For example, 48% were involved in group sports, 77% attended Sunday school, 47% were involved in music classes, and 87% engaged in play activities with people outside the family. Table 7 indicates the number of hours that the students in these families spent in contact with persons other than their parents. For example, they spend, on average, 10 hours per week in contact with non-family adults and 11 hours per week with non-sibling children.

More specific data were collected on the church-related activities of the students. Eighty-five percent of the students attended church worship services 4 to 7 times per month, while

2.9% never attended church worship services. Seventy-two percent of these children attended Sunday school classes 4 to 7 times per

Activity	Percent of Students*
Play with People Outside the Family	87
Field Trips	84
Sunday School	77
Group Sports	48
Music Classes	47
Classes with Students Outside the Home	42
Bible Clubs	35
Ministry	34
Volunteer Work with People	33
4-H	14
Ballet/Dance Classes	10
Scouts	8
Other Activities	25

* Percent given is valid percent from a base of 3,582 students currently home educated.

Table 8. Social activities of home educated children.

month, while 4.7% never attended Sunday school class. Thirty-seven percent attended church youth group 4 to 7 times per month, while 15% never attended church youth groups. The Appendix contains more detailed data regarding church-related activities.

The average number of years in home education was 4.8 (SD = 2.80, N = 3,480) for those students who were at least five years of age and were being home educated.

The instrument requested that the children respond to 4 items about their lives. Their responses indicated that 46% spend no time playing video or computer games during weekdays, while 42% play them less than one hour per weekday (Table 9). Eighteen percent watch no television or videotapes during weekdays, while 35% watch them less than one hour per weekday and 27% watch 1 to less than 2 hours per weekday (Table 10).

Time Spent	Percent Weekdays	Percent Weekends
None	46	41
Less than 1 hr/day	42	38
1 to less than 2 hr/day	10	13
2 to less than 3 hr/day	2	6
3 to less than 5 hr/day	<1	2
5 or more hr/day	<1	<1

Table 9. Time spent playing video or computer games. (n = 3,582 students) (Total may not equal 100 due to rounding error.)

Time Spent	Percent Weekdays	Percent Weekends
None	18	10
Less than 1 hr/day	35	23
1 to less than 2 hr/day	27	27
2 to less than 3 hr/day	15	25
3 to less than 5 hr/day	5	13
5 or more hr/day	1	3

Table 10. Time spent watching TV or videotapes. (n = 3,582 students) (Total may not equal 100 due to rounding error.)

Grade Level	Percent
Kindergarten	8.6
1	10.2
2	10.6
3	9.8
4	10.7
5	9.3
6	9.2
7	9.7
8	7.3
9	5.3
10	3.9
11	2.9
12	1.9
13	.4
14	.1
15	.0
16	.0
Total	99.9 *

Mean = 4.8, Median = 5.0, Mode = 4.0, n = 3,199
* May not equal 100 due to rounding error.

Table 11. Grade levels of students being home educated.

Kind of Curriculum	Percent That Marked This Option*
Parent-Designed (major components hand-picked by parents)	71.1
Satellite School (as source)	3.0
Home School Program from Local Private School	0.7
No Particular Curriculum Plan	6.5
Complete Curricular Package	23.8

* A parent could mark more than one option per child. These data are based on 3,582 students.

Table 12. Kind of curriculum used for teaching the children at home.

Curriculum	Freq.	%
A Beka	278	31.2
Alaska State Dept. Educ.	1	.1
Alpha Omega	38	4.3
Basic Education (ACE)	34	3.8
BJU Press	146	16.4
Calvert School	41	4.6
Christian Liberty Acad.	99	11.1
Christian Light	16	1.8
Covenant Home Curric.	10	1.1
Hewitt Child Develop.	17	1.9
Oak Meadow Education	19	2.1
Seton School Home Study	34	3.8
Summit Christian Academy	1	.1
Sycamore Tree	2	.2
Other Complete Curric.	155	17.4
Total	891	99.9

Table 13. Complete curricular packages used for 891 students.

Students' Academic Achievement

A number of findings were observed related to the students in this study who took standardized achievement tests. Some of the findings are presented in this section.

General findings

Of 3,466 students who were being home educated, and for whom relevant data were available, 53.7% took a standardized achievement or college aptitude test during the past 24 months.

Table 14 indicates the types of standardized academic achievement tests that were used for 1,952 students. The most frequently used (by 37%) test was the *Iowa Test of Basic Skills*, while 30% took the *Stanford Achievement Test*. The average age of students taking achievement tests was 11.00 ($SD = 2.89$, $n = 1864$) and the average grade level of the tests was 5.43 ($SD = 2.89$, $n = 1824$). The person who administered the test was a public school teacher in 10.3% of the cases, a private school teacher in 12.3% of the cases, the parent in 43.9% of the cases, or some other administrator (such as a home education support group member or a qualified test administrator) in 33.5% of the cases. Copies of test results from the test publisher or test administrator were submitted for 77% of the students.

The students scored, on the average, at the following percentiles on standardized achievement tests: (a) total reading, 87th, (b) total language, 80th, (c) total math, 82nd, (d) total listening, 85th, (e) science, 84th, (f) social studies, 85th, (g) study skills, 81st, (h) basic battery (typically, reading, language, and mathematics), 85th, and (i) complete battery (all subject areas in which student was tested), 87th. (Note: The average score on standardized tests for the norm group, largely conventional school students, in all of the preceding categories is the 50th percentile. See Appendix A, the normal curve with percentile equivalents.)

Test Name	Freq.	%
Iowa Test of Basic Skills	728	37.3
Stanford Achievement Test	581	29.8
California Achievement Test	304	15.6
Comprehensive Test of Basic Skills	130	6.7
Metropolitan Achievement Test	52	2.7
Tests of Achievement and Proficiency	3	.2
Other	154	7.9
Total	1952	100.2

Table 14. Standardized tests used for children taught at home.

Effect sizes ranged from a low of .85 (language) to a high of 1.15 (reading). Table 15 presents summary statistics on academic achievement. Not all students were tested in all subject areas; therefore, sample sizes varied.

These home educated students' achievement test scores were significantly higher than the national average of the 50th percentile in all areas: total reading, $t(1593) = 54.51$, $p< .001$; total language, $t(1485) = 36.80$, $p< .001$; total listening, $t(579) = 29.71$, $p< .001$; total math, $t(1612) = 41.41$, $p< .001$; science, $t(1132) = 41.05$, $p< .001$; social studies, $t(1098) = 41.61$, $p< .001$; study skills, $t(915) = 32.34$, $p< .001$; basic battery, $t(1337) = 47.21$, $p< .001$; complete battery, $t(1091) = 45.91$, $p< .001$. Complete one-sample t-test statistics are provided in Appendix C.

The reading, language, and math test score data were examined to determine whether low scores were ever reported by the parents. In reading, scores at or below the 16th percentile (-1.0 standard deviation) were reported for 26 students. In language, scores at or below the 16th percentile were reported for 39 students. In math, scores at or below the 16th percentile were reported for 35 students. The lowest score possible, the 1st percentile, was reported for both language and math.

Figure 11 shows how these test scores compare to standardized test norm groups. The maximum score possible is the 99th percentile (or a z-score of 2.33) and the minimum score possible is the 1st percentile (or a z-score of -2.33). The national average for the norm group (typically from conventional schools) is the 50th percentile (or a z-score of 0). The home educated in this study typically scored about the 84th percentile (or a z-score of 1.00).

Variable	Natl. %ile*	Mean z	SD z	N
Reading, Total	87	1.15	.84	1594
Listening, Total	85	1.05	.85	580
Language, Total	80	.85	.90	1486
Math, Total	82	.90	.87	1613
Science	84	1.00	.82	1133
Social Studies	85	1.03	.82	1099
Study Skills	81	.87	.81	916
Basic Battery	85	1.05	.81	1338
Complete Battery	87	1.11	.80	1092

(Note: A given z-score may have slightly different percentiles associated with it due to lack of precision in conversion.)

Natl. %ile = National Percentile; Mean z = Mean z-score; SD z = Standard Deviation z-score; N = Sample Size

* All means for the home educated were significantly higher ($p < .001$) than the 50%ile national average (see narrative text).

Table 15. Summary of home educated students' standardized achievement test scores. (Note: The national average for public school students is the 50th percentile in all areas.)

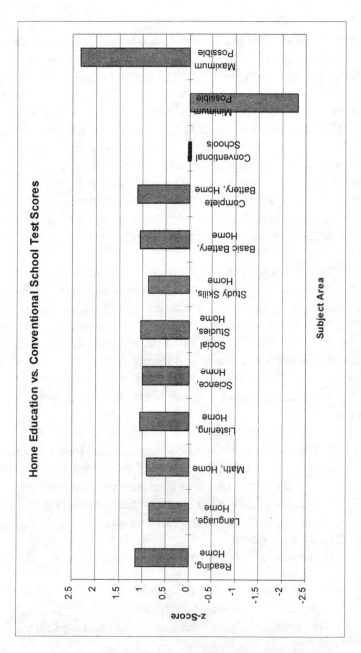

Figure 11. Home education and conventional school average achievement test scores. The maximum possible is 2.33 and minimum possible is -2.33. The national average is a z-score of 0.00 (i.e., 50th percentile).

Variables that explain achievement scores

Multiple regression analysis (stepwise) was used to determine whether any of several independent variables explained significant amounts of variance in students' total reading, total language, total mathematics, and complete battery on standardized achievement tests. The researcher decided that only these four dependent variables would be used for two reasons. First, past research that has explored many independent variables and test scores have shown that few independent variables explain statistically significant and practically significant amounts of variance in home educated students' test scores (Rakestraw, 1988; Ray, 1990b, 1992b, 1994; Russell, 1994; Wartes, 1990a). Second, reducing the number of dependent variables reduces the number of statistical tests to be performed which reduces multiple error rate (Good, 1984).

Furthermore, the researcher originally planned to include the student's age and the degree of structure in the home education environment as independent variables. Analyses of collinearity between independent variables, however, gave evidence that these two variables should be excluded from analyses in order to increase the likelihood of valid and meaningful multiple regression results.

The independent variables entered into the regression analyses were the:

 (a) highest formal education level attained by the father,
 (b) highest formal education level attained by the mother,
 (c) teacher certification status of the father (i.e., whether the father had ever been a certified teacher),
 (d) teacher certification status of the mother (i.e., whether the mother had ever been a certified teacher),
 (e) family income,
 (f) amount of money spent on the home education of the student,
 (g) legal status of the family (Table 3),
 (h) gender of the student,
 (i) the number of years the student was home educated,

(j) the extent to which the family visits public libraries, and

(k) the time spent in formal education activities, and

(l) the age at which the student's formal education commenced.

Seven of the 12 independent variables did not explain statistically significant amounts of variance in students' test scores. These 7 were (1) father's certification status, (2) mother's certification status, (3) family income, (4) money spent on home education, (5) legal status of family, (6) time spent in formal educational activities, and (7) age at which began formal education.

Only 5 of the 12 independent variables explained statistically significant amounts of variance in students' test scores for any of the subject areas explored. The five significant variables were father's education level, mother's education level, years taught at home, gender of the student, and number of visits to the public library. The maximum amount of variance in the test scores that any one of these independent variables explained was 5.0% (and this was by father's education level for the complete battery scores).

Father's education level, years the student was taught at home, and number of visits to the public library explained statistically significant amounts of variance in *total reading* scores (Table 16). The amount of variance explained, however, was relatively small. The strongest predictor of the reading score was the father's education level. The reading z-score would be .048 higher per additional year of the father's formal education. This would be .02 to 1.9 percentiles of reading score per year of father's education (in this study). Father's educational level explained only 2.5% of the variance in reading scores. The number of years home educated and number of visits to the public library per month were positively related to reading scores.

Independent Variable	R^2 Adjusted	R^2 Change
Father's Education Level	.02472	
Years Home Educated	.03385	.009
Visits Public Library	.03825	.004

Analysis of Variance

	DF	SS	MS
Regression	3	38.01040	12.67013
Residual	1331	902.59261	.67813

F =   18.68390   Signif F = .0000

------------------------ Variables in the Equation ------------------------

Variable	B	SE B	Beta	T	Sig T
FATHED	.047810	.007834	.163971	6.103	.0000
HOMEYRS	.033061	.008748	.101579	3.779	.0002
LIBRPUB	.026689	.010019	.071580	. 2.664	.0078
(Constant)	.140582	.138328		1.016	.3097

Table 16. Coefficients of determination, analysis of variance, and other statistics regarding the multiple regression for **Total Reading** test scores with three significant independent variables (i.e., father's formal education level, years taught at home, and number of visits to the public library).

Father's education level, gender of the student, mother's education level, and number of years home educated explained statistically significant amounts of variance in the *total language* scores (Table 17). The amount of variance explained, however, was relatively small. Father's education was the strongest predictor. The student's language z-score would be .054 (or .01 to 2.2 percentiles) higher per additional year of father's formal education. The number of years home educated and mother's education level were positively related to language scores. Females scored somewhat higher in language than did males.

Independent Variable	R^2 Adjusted	R^2 Change
Father's Education Level	.04149	
Gender of Student	.06103	.020
Mother's Education Level	.06568	.005
Years Home Educated	.07014	.004

Analysis of Variance

	DF	SS	MS
Regression	4	72.55888	18.13972
Residual	1234	919.40706	.74506

F = 24.34658   Signif F = .0000

------------------------ Variables in the Equation -------------------------

Variable	B	SE B	Beta	T	Sig T
FATHED	.054312	.009601	.174736	5.657	.0000
MOTHED	.036936	.013567	.084083	2.722	.0066
GENDER	-.253990	.049130	-.141909	-5.170	.0000
HOMEYRS	.025061	.009519	.072232	2.633	.0086
(Constant)	-.547542	.196476		-2.787	.0054

Table 17. Coefficients of determination, analysis of variance, and other statistics regarding the multiple regression for **Total Language** test scores with four significant independent variables (i.e., father's formal education level, gender of student, mother's formal education level, and years taught at home,).

Mother's education level, father's education level, and gender of student explained statistically significant amounts of variance in the *total math* scores (Table 18). The amount of variance explained, however, was relatively small. Mother's education was the strongest predictor. The student's language z-score would be .056 (or .02 to 2.2 percentiles) higher per additional year of mother's formal education. The father's education level was positively related to math scores. In addition, males scored somewhat higher in math than did females.

Independent Variable	R^2 Adjusted	R^2 Change
Mother's Education Level	.03577	
Father's Education Level	.04749	.012
Gender of Student	.05487	.007

Analysis of Variance

	DF	SS	MS
Regression	3	58.81049	19.60350
Residual	1347	973.51453	.72273

F = 27.12431 Signif F = .0000

------------------------ Variables in the Equation ------------------------

Variable	B	SE B	Beta	T	Sig T
FATHED	.037344	.009053	.122984	4.125	.0000
MOTHED	.056156	.012794	.130859	4.389	.0000
GENDER	.157257	.046314	.089939	3.395	.0007
(Constant)	-.585768	.177116		-3.307	.0010

Table 18. Coefficients of determination, analysis of variance, and other statistics regarding the multiple regression for **Total Math** test scores with three significant independent variables (i.e., mother's formal education level, father's formal education level, and gender of student).

Father's education level and mother's education level explained statistically significant amounts of variance in the *complete battery* scores (Table 19). Father's education was the strongest predictor. The student's language z-score would be .050 (or .01 to 2.0 percentiles) higher per additional year of father's formal education. The mother's education level was positively related to complete battery scores.

Detailed data regarding correlation coefficients between the test scores and the interval-data independent variables mentioned in the preceding section on multiple regression are available in the Appendix C.

Independent Variable | R^2 Adjusted | R^2 Change
Father's Education Level | .04997 |
Mother's Education Level | .05621 | .006

Analysis of Variance

	DF	SS	MS
Regression	2	33.70664	16.85332
Residual	908	544.61842	.59980

$F = 28.09823$ Signif $F = .0000$

------------------------ Variables in the Equation ------------------------

Variable	B	SE B	Beta	T	Sig T
FATHED	050286	.010042	.181658	5.007	.0000
MOTHED	.037568	.014193	.096028	2.647	.0083
(Constant)	-.232221	.195413		-1.188	.2350

Table 19. Coefficients of determination, analysis of variance, and other statistics regarding the multiple regression for **Complete Battery** test scores with two significant independent variables (i.e., father's formal education level and mother's formal education level).

Degree of Regulation of Home Education in the State and Test Scores

An analysis of variance (ANOVA) was conducted to test whether the degree of regulation of home education by a state has an effect on students' basic battery test scores. States were categorized as having either low regulation, moderate regulation, or high regulation (Table 20). Low regulation was defined as no state requirement on the part of the home school parents to initiate any contact with the state. Moderate regulation was defined as the state requiring home school parents to send to the state notification or achievement test scores and/or evaluation of the student's learning by a professional. High regulation was defined as the state requiring home school parents to send to the state notification or achievement test scores and/or evaluation by a professional and, in addition, having other requirements (e.g., curriculum approval by the state, teacher qualifications of parents, or home visits by state officials). There was no significant difference between students' scores in the three groups.

Analysis of Variance

Source	D.F.	Sum of Squares	Mean Squares	F Ratio	F Prob.
Between Groups	2	.1179	.0589	.0898	.9141
Within Groups	1236	811.3733	.6565		
Total	1238	811.4911			

Group	Count	Mean	S.D.	S.E.	95% Conf Int
Grp 1	187	1.0721	.8437	.0617	.9504 to 1.1938
Grp 2	758	1.0515	.7921	.0288	.9950 to 1.1079
Grp 3	294	1.0711	.8343	.0487	.9753 to 1.1668
Total	1239	1.0592	.8096	.0230	1.0141 to 1.1043

Grp 1 = Low Regulation = states of ID, IL, IN, MI, MO, NJ, OK, and TX.
Grp 2 = Moderate Regulation = states of AK, AL, AZ, CA, CO, CT, DC, DE, FL, GA, HI, IA, KS, KY, LA, MD, MS, MT, NC, NE, NH, NM, OH, OR, SC, SD, TN, VA, WI, and WY.
Grp 3 = High Regulation = states of AR, MA, ME, MN, ND, NV, NY, PA, RI, UT, VT, WA, and WV.

Table 20. Basic battery test scores compared according to degree of regulation of home education by the state.

Test Administrator and Test Scores

The researcher tested whether there was a difference between basic battery scores of students based on who administered the test. All four groups had scores that were above average. An analysis of variance (ANOVA) and an LSD multiple range test revealed that there was no significant difference in basic battery scores when students were tested by public school teachers ($M =$ 85th %ile) compared to when they were administered tests by their parents (M = 88th %ile) (see Appendix C for ANOVA table and LSD results). Scores of students who were tested by their parents, however, were significantly higher than scores of those tested by private school teachers ($M =$ 81st %ile) and by others ($M =$ 84th %ile).

Use of Computer for Education of the Child and Test Scores

A comparison was made between achievement scores of children who used a computer for their education and those who did not. These *t-tests* were done for reading, language, math, science, and social studies. The only subject for which there was a significant difference was reading; those using computers for their education scored higher ($M =$ 88%ile) than those not using computers ($M =$ 85%ile), $t(1554) = 2.59$, $p < .01$. (See Appendix for detailed tables.)

Table 21 provides a summary of all of the statistical analyses that explored the relationship between the several independent variables and various achievement test scores.

Independent Variable	Reading	Language	Math	Science	Social Studies	Basic Battery	Complete Battery
Father's Education	Very small Slight	Very small Low	Very small Slight	n/a	n/a	n/a	Very small Low
Mother's Education	No	Very small Slight	Very small Slight	n/a	n/a	n/a	Very small Slight
Father is Certified Teacher	No	No	No	n/a	n/a	n/a	No
Mother is Certified Teacher	No	No	No	n/a	n/a	n/a	No
Family Income	No	No	No	n/a	n/a	n/a	No
Money Spent on Education	No	No	No	n/a	n/a	n/a	No
Legal Status	No	No	No	n/a	n/a	n/a	No
Gender	No	Slight Girls higher	Slight Boys higher	n/a		n/a	No
Years Home Educated	Slight, Positive	Slight, Positive	No	n/a	n/a	n/a	No
Use of Libraries	Slight, Positive	No	No	n/a	n/a	n/a	No
Time in Formal Instruction	No	No	No	n/a	n/a	n/a	No
Age Began Formal Instruction	No	No	No	n/a	n/a	n/a	No
Degree of State Regulation	n/a	n/a	n/a	n/a	n/a	No	n/a
Test Administrator	n/a	n/a	n/a	n/a	n/a	Slight Mixed results	n/a
Use of Computer	Slight, Positive	No	No	No	No	n/a	n/a

Table 21. Summary of statistical analyses showing which of the selected independent variables were statistically significantly related to achievement test scores. The qualitative descriptors "slight" and "low" are used according to Guilford's definitions (cited in Sprinthall, 1990, p. 208). Guilford also used "moderate," "high," and "very high," but none of these apply to the relationships in this table. The symbol "n/a" means "not applicable—no statistical test was done."

Graduates of Home Education

The survey also asked questions about home educated students who had "graduated from high school" (n = 232). Students who had been home educated and had graduated from their secondary school academic studies were home schooled, on average, 6.9 years (SD = .218, n = 216, median = 7.0). Immediately after high school graduation from home education, 25.4% went to a four-year college on a full-time basis, 16.8% went into full-time employment, 12.1% went into part-time higher education and part-time employment, 10.3% took part-time employment, 8.2% went to community college, and the remainder said they did other things. More detail is presented in Table 22. A further analysis was done of those who selected the "other" category.

Activity	Freq.	%
Junior or Community College	19	8.2
Four-Year College, Full-Time	59	25.4
Trade School	4	1.7
Business School	1	.4
Full-Time Employment	39	16.8
Part-Time Employment	24	10.3
Part-Time Higher Ed. & Part-Time Employment	28	12.1
Military	1	.4
Other	57	24.6
Total	232	99.9

Table 22. Post-secondary activities of home educated students.

For the 25% who did "other" things, reported activities and approximate percentages were as follow: some form of formal postsecondary education that was sometimes with part-time work (35%), apprenticeship (e.g., midwifery, Advanced Training Institute of Oak Brook, IL) (20%), more home study (13%), employment (9.3%), religious missions or ministry (9.3%), homemaking or marriage preparation (7.4%), and miscellaneous (5.6%). Overall, then, about 49% went directly on to some form of postsecondary academic study.

Another way to summarize what these graduates did soon after their secondary or high school years is to only consider those who went on to some form of postsecondary education, full-time or part-time, or into employment. This analysis did not include those who went into the military, religious missions, religious ministry, volunteer work, *et cetera*. This analysis revealed that 69% went on to postsecondary education and 31% into employment.

Longitudinal Findings

Families ($n = 275$) and children who were involved in both Ray's 1990 nationwide study and this study were compared on several factors (Table 23). It appears that the differences are minor with respect to factors such as father's education level, mother's education level, family income, cost per child to home educate, and number of visits to public libraries. The average number of years that children were home educated, however, increased from 3.1 to 6.0.

Table 24 shows the curriculum used by families in Ray's 1990 nationwide study and during this study. There was a slight difference in that a parent-designed curriculum was used 67% of the time in 1990 and 71% of the time in this study. The greatest change was in the use of a complete curriculum package; it decreased from 31% in 1990 to 24% in this study. The choice options presented to parents, however, were slightly different in the two studies.

For those students for whom there were achievement test scores available in the 1990 study and this study (Table 25), paired *t-tests* were done to compare their scores several years apart (see Appendix C for detailed statistical tables). Scores were available for reading, listening, language, math, science, social studies, basic battery, and complete battery. The *t-value* was not statistically significant in any of these comparisons. That is to say, for each subject area and testing category, these students' scores were statistically the same in the two studies. In both studies, the scores were well above the national average of conventional school students.

Variable Study	1990 Study	Current Study
Father's Education Level	15.30	15.51
Mother's Education Level	14.45	14.53
Income, Total Household		
(Median, dollars, not adjusted)	35,000 to 49,999	43,000
Years Child Home Educated	3.09	6.04
Visits to Public Library per Month	3.27	2.71
Cost Per Child Per Year to Home		
Educate (dollars, not adjusted)	465.29	499.01

Table 23. Comparison of selected descriptive characteristics of families and children who participated in both the 1990 study and this study. Means are shown unless otherwise noted. Overall, $n = 275$ families; sample sizes above varied due to missing data.

	Percent Option Marked *	
Kind of Curriculum	1990	This Study
Parent-Designed (major components		
hand-picked by parents)	67.4	71.1
Satellite School (as source)	5.1	3.0
Home School Program from Local		
Private School	1.3	0.7
No Particular Curriculum Plan	**	6.5
Complete Curricular Package	31.4	23.8

* A parent could mark more than one option per child so total may exceed 100.

** This response choice was not offered to parents in the 1990 study.

Table 24. Kind of curriculum used for teaching the children at home in Ray's 1990 study and the present study.

Subject	1990 Study %ile	N	Current Study %ile	N
Reading	87	218	86	358
Language	83	170	80	341
Math	83	222	80	369
Listening	90	53	82	120
Science	87	72	81	267
Social Studies	87	72	83	257
Basic Battery	86	147	84	313
Complete Battery	86	147	85	237

Table 25. Summary of academic achievement test scores of students who participated in both the 1990 study and this study. (National percentiles and sample sizes are given. Data were not available for study skills for both years.)

4

Conclusions and Commentary

The closing portion of this report provides a synopsis of the findings of this study and some reflective and interpretive commentary.

Families

Data were gathered on 1,657 home schooling families and their 5,402 children from every state, the District of Columbia, and three United States territories. The seven states that each comprised at least 3% of the sample were Texas (6.5%), California (6.3%), Virginia (4.8%), Washington (4.6%), Ohio (4.2%), New York (3.6%), and Pennsylvania (3%).

On average, these families were much larger than the average for the United States. They had 3.3 children and 98% of the families for whom data were available were headed by married couples. The average number of children in married-couple families in the United States was 1.8 in 1990 (United States Bureau of the Census, 1994a, p. 66). Home school families, therefore, have 83% more children than the average. In 1990, 73% of children under the age of 18 in the United States lived with a married couple.

Fathers were clearly the main breadwinners in these families. Thirty-four percent of fathers were professionals such as accountants, engineers, bankers, ministers, dentists, doctors, lawyers, and college teachers. Eleven percent were small business owners. Eighty-eight percent of the mothers were homemakers/home educators and only 16% of the mothers worked outside the home. Mothers who worked outside the home did so for an average of 14 hours per week.

Thirty-one percent of the fathers and 34% of the mothers had earned a bachelor's degree as their highest formal educational attainment. Fifteen percent of the fathers and 8% of the mothers had earned a master's degree. The highest educational attainment was high school for 23% of the fathers and 26% of the mothers. In contrast, the highest educational attainment is high school for 34% of adults in the general public (United States Bureau of the Census, 1996b). Only 16% of the general public had earned a bachelor's degree, and only 5% had earned a master's degree. In summary, about 53% of home educators had earned a bachelor's degree or higher; only about 24% of the general public had done so. This population of home educators had a noticeably higher level of educational attainment than that of the general public.

The median annual family income of home school families was $43,000 in 1995. The median income for all married-couple families in the United States in 1995 was $47,062 (United States Bureau of the Census, 1996a). These home education families had noticeably lower incomes than did married-couple families across America.

On the other hand, married-couple families across the United States with the wife not in the paid labor force had a median income in 1995 of $32,375 (United States Bureau of the Census, 1996a). This is relevant because the majority of the mothers in this study (84%) did not work outside of the home. It is not known, however, how many of these mothers worked from home-based businesses so it is not known what percent were in the paid labor force. More data would have to be collected to make a careful analysis of the topic of incomes as they compare to precisely similar families across the United States. These home education families had median incomes that were lower than those of all married-couple families across America, but were higher than those of married-couple families with the wife not in the paid labor force.

The parents spent, on average, $546 per child per year for home education (and the median was $400). State schools spent an average of $5,325 per student (pre-kindergarten through the 12th grade) during school year 1993-94 (United States Department of Education, National Center for Education Statistics, 1996). This cost in state schools did not include construction, equipment and debt financing. The highest per-pupil expenditure was $9,075 in New Jersey; the lowest was $3,206 in Utah. It is clear that the direct costs of public (state-run) schooling in the United States are at least 975% (or about 10 times as much) of what the home education families in this study spent on educational materials and services.

The findings of this study and further investigation (e.g., contact with curriculum providers who provided marketing data) led the researcher to the estimate that 1,226,000 (±15%) K-12 students were being home educated during the 1996-1997 academic year. (This estimate is close to Ray's 1996 estimate; cf., Lines, 1996.) Based on this estimate, this would represent $6.5 billion (±15%) that United States taxpayers did not have to spend on public education, not including what would have to be spent on construction, equipment, and debt financing for these extra students. These figures on the cost of home education are similar to what Ray (1990b) reported. (Some observers have argued that the lost opportunity wage of one of the parents is also a cost of home education. This is, however, a very complex and debatable issue.)

About 90% of the parents claim Christianity as their religious affiliation (e.g., evangelical, fundamental, Catholic). Most of these are what the author names as basic biblical Christians. About 5% of the parents were Roman Catholic. Another 1% to 2% were represented by each of the categories of Mormon (Latter-Day Saints)/Jehovah's Witness and New Age/Eastern religion. Other religions, such as Unitarian Universalism, Zen Buddhism, and pantheism were represented. Eighty-three percent of the fathers and 86% of the mothers who responded to the questionnaire item claimed to be "born again" Christians.

Ninety-six percent of the parents were white (not Hispanic) in terms of race/ethnicity. All minority categories, however, were represented in this study.

Eighty-six percent of the families had a computer in their home. Computers were used for the education of 84% of the children of these families. The average number of visits to any kind of library was 3.8 per month. Public libraries were visited 3 to 4 times per month by 32% of the families.

Mothers did 88% of the formal instruction of their children, fathers did just under 10% of the formal instruction, and other people did a little more than 3% of the formal instruction of the students. Only 6% of the fathers and 15% of the mothers had ever been certified teachers.

About 67% of the children's grandparents supported the families' practice of home education. About 22% of the grandparents were neutral toward the home education of their grandchildren. Only about 11% of the grandparents were opposed to home schooling.

Children

Many findings about children were made. Some of the data simply corroborate the findings of earlier research while other data shed new light on children and youth who are home educated.

General Demographics

On average, each child in these home school families had 2 to 3 siblings; 28% had 2 and 20% had 3. Thirty-eight percent of the families had 4 or more children. As mentioned earlier, these families were much larger than the average for the United States. They had 3.3 children and 98% of the families for whom data were available were headed by married couples. The average number of children in married-couple families in the United States was only 1.8 in 1990 (United States Bureau of the Census, 1994a, p. 66). These home educated children lived in relatively large families.

The average age of the children who were being home educated in the families was 10.5 years. Late fourth or early fifth grade was the average grade level of the students who were being home educated.

The average number of years in home education was 5 for those students who were at least five years of age and were being home educated. Parents planned to home educate 76% of all of the currently-home educated children through the 12th grade. Their plans were to home educate 10% of them through college. The parents in this study plan to home educate their children a little longer (M = grade 11.83) than did the parents in Ray's (1990b) study (M = grade10.88). This author thinks that a careful look at the data (if one could examine Ray's raw data) would indicate that this change is due to the fact that more parents in the current study than in the 1990 study planned to educate their children through the high school years. An increasing number of parents appear to be more committed to long-term home education.

Grades Kindergarten (K) through 8 included 85.4% of the students while grades 9 through 12 included 14% of the students. Across the United States in 1992, 73.2% of K-12 students were in grades K through 8, while 26.8% were in grades 9 through 12. The home education sample in this study is slightly positively skewed. That is, there is a moderately disproportionate number of younger students being home educated. For the sake of another comparison, Ray (1990b) found that 87% of the home education students were in grades 1 through 8 while 77% in the present study were in grades 1 through 8. It appears that the distribution in the present study more closely resembles the national norm than did the distribution of students in the 1990 study.

The male-to-female ratio of the home educated students was one-to-one. This basically matches national United States demographics.

Ninety-five percent of the students were non-Hispanic white in terms of their race/ethnic group. The categories of non-Hispanic Black, Hispanic, Asian/Pacific Islander/Oriental, and American

Indian/Alaskan Native were all represented. In 1994, 78.5% of K-12 students in the United States were white (United States Bureau of the Census, 1994a). Without performing a careful analysis of all possible factors, then, it appears that white students are disproportionately represented in this home schooling sample. This is consistent with other researchers' findings (e.g., Burns, 1993; Mayberry, Knowles, Ray, & Marlow, 1995; Ray, 1994). Researchers have done little to ascertain whether these findings are representative of who is actually involved in home education. Research findings and the experience of many who are very familiar with home education suggest that minority races/ethnicities are underrepresented in home schooling.

The reasons for the home education population being overrepresented by non-Hispanic whites have not been studied. This author can think of several possible explanations. First, it is possible that the middle-income and "white" constitution of the home education population appears uninviting, for various reasons, to members of other racial groups. A corollary to this possibility is that perhaps home educators have not, in a concentrated way, recruited persons of minority groups to participate in home schooling. This is, however, beginning to happen. For example, in the fall of 1996, a group of home school leaders met in the Washington, D.C. area to develop strategy regarding how to reach and explain the home education option to minority and low-income families (Home School Legal Defense Association, 1996, p. 9). One explanation of the meetings follows: "White and black home schoolers in the DC metropolitan area have been meeting together since April, 1996 to find ways for the existing home school community in the suburbs to serve the newer generation of home schoolers in the city" (Somerville, 1996).

Second, it may be that members of minority groups have been told for generations that state-run, "inclusive" schools are their most-likely route to success—and now they believe it more than do other groups. Third, majority-group home educators may be, in some fashion, discriminating against others—there is, however, no research evidence supporting this speculation and this author has not encountered any significant evidence of this among the home education community.

Finally, perhaps minority parents are subtly pressured to keep or place their children in conventional schools by their own groups' peers when they openly consider or choose the unconventional route of home education. There may be many more reasons for the underrepresentation of minority groups. Despite the largely non-Hispanic white makeup of current home education, at least some leaders in minority groups think that home education is good for the families within their minority groups. An African-American woman who served at a high level in an eastern state's department of health and human resources (and who asked to remain anonymous with respect to this comment) said to this researcher and others that, "Home education is the best way for minority [including African American] families to help their children succeed in America" (personal communication, 1994).

Curriculum and Extracurricular Activities

Parents used a self-designed curriculum (i.e., the major components were hand-picked or selected by the parents, often from various curriculum suppliers) for 71% of the students, a complete curricular package (i.e., included language, social studies, mathematics, and science material for a full year) for 24% of the students, no particular curriculum plan for 6% of the students, a local private school's home education program for 1% of the students, and a satellite school (i.e., materials from a private school or educational organization that works with the home educated at a distance) for 3% of the students.

Children in these families were engaged in a wide variety of social activities. For example, 87% engaged in play activities with people outside the family, 77% participated in Sunday school, 48% were involved in group sports, and 47% were involved in music classes. These children spent, on average, 10 hours per week in contact with non-family adults. It is clear, as other researchers have pointed out, that these children are not socially isolated. Further, it appears that the amount and quality of their social interaction does not inhibit their social and psychological development (Carson,

1990; Chatham-Carpenter, 1994; Delahooke, 1986; Hedin, 1991; Johnson, 1991; Kelly, 1991; Knowles & Muchmore, 1995; Medlin, 1994; Montgomery, 1989; Shyers, 1992; Smedley, 1992; Taylor, 1986; Tillman, 1995).

Children reported that 46% of them spent *no* time playing video or computer games during weekdays, while 42% played them less than one hour per weekday. Eighteen percent watched *no* television or videotapes during weekdays, while 35% watched less than one hour per weekday and 27% watched 1 to less than 2 hours per weekday. The time they spent playing video and computer games and watching TV or videos is probably much less than what is spent by their peers in public schools. For example, only 4% of students in the upper grades in public schools watched no television or videotapes during weekdays, while 14% watched less than one hour per weekday, 20% watched 1 to less than 2 hours per day, and 40% watched 2 hours or more (United States Department of Education, Office of Educational Research and Improvement, 1996a). Research on the relationship between television viewing and academic achievement has yielded mixed results (Hagborg, 1995; Smith, 1992; Williams, Haertel, Haertel, & Walberg, 1982 [cited in Smith, 1992]).

Students' Academic Achievement

These home educated students fared very well on standardized academic achievement tests. In addition, very few demographic or learning environment factors were significantly related to their achievement. Possible reasons for this strong performance will be explored later in this report.

About half of the students in these families took a standardized achievement or college aptitude test during the past 24 months. Both the *Iowa Test of Basic Skills* and the *Stanford Achievement Test* were used by about one-third of the students. The average age of students taking achievement tests was 11 and the average grade level of the tests was 5.

The students scored, on the average, at the following percentiles on standardized academic achievement tests: (a) total reading, 87th, (b) total language, 80th, (c) total math, 82nd, (d) total listening, 85th, (e) science, 84th, (f) social studies, 85th, (g) study skills, 81st, (h) basic battery (typically, reading, language, and mathematics), 85th, and (i) complete battery (all subject areas in which student was tested), 87th. These are very high scores considering the fact that the average score on standardized tests for the norm group, conventional school students, in all of the preceding categories is the 50th percentile. All of these subtest scores were statistically significantly higher than the national average. Perhaps more impressive were the large effect sizes. These home educated students performed, on average, from .85 standard deviation (in language) to a high of 1.15 standard deviations (in reading) above the national average. Researchers consider effect sizes larger than .33 to have *practical significance* (Borg & Gall, 1989, p. 7). All of these effect sizes are, practically speaking, impressive.

The home educated in this study typically scored about the 84th percentile. These scores are consistent with those found by Ray (1990b) and many other researchers across America and in Canada (Priesnitz & Priesnitz , 1990; Ray, 1994).

There was evidence that some home schooling parents were willing to report low test scores. In each of the academic areas of reading, language, and math, scores at or below the 16th percentile (-1.0 standard deviation) were reported for 26 to 39 students. The lowest score possible, the 1st percentile, was reported in both language and math.

Variables that explain achievement scores

Several analyses were conducted to determine which independent variables were significantly related to academic achievement.

Only 5 of the 12 independent variables used in multiple regression explained statistically significant amounts of variance in students' test scores for any of the subject areas explored. The five significant variables were father's education level, mother's education level, years taught at home, gender of the student, and frequency of visits to the public library. The maximum amount of variance in the test scores that any one of these independent variables explained was 5.0% (and this was by father's education level for the complete battery scores).

Father's education level, years the student was taught at home, and number of visits to the public library were all positively related to and explained statistically significant amounts of variance in *total reading* scores. All together, however, these three variables explained only 3.8% of the variance in reading scores. That is, less than 4% of the total variance (i.e., total = 100%) in reading scores is dependent on variations in these three factors. This explanatory power is, practically speaking, insignificant.

Father's education level (i.e., a positive relationship), gender of the student (i.e., females outperformed males), mother's education level (i.e., a positive relationship), and number of years home educated (i.e., a positive relationship) explained statistically significant amounts of variance in the *total language* scores. All together, however, these four variables explained only 7.0% of the variance in reading scores. This explanatory power is, practically speaking, quite insignificant.

Mother's education level (i.e., a positive relationship), father's education level (i.e., a positive relationship), and gender of student (i.e., males outperformed females) explained statistically significant amounts of variance in the *total math* scores. All together, however, these three variables explained only 5.5% of the variance in math scores. This explanatory power is, practically speaking, rather insignificant.

Father's education level and mother's education level were positively related to and explained statistically significant amounts of variance in the *complete battery* scores. All together, however, these two variables explained only 5.6% of the variance in complete battery scores. This explanatory power is, practically speaking, quite insignificant.

It could be argued that the scores of these home educated students are relatively high and homogeneous. The argument would say that this range restriction, therefore, would reduce the likelihood of finding statistically significant independent variables. In some cases in this study, range restriction probably exists but it would be very difficult (if at all possible) to estimate the true correlations adjusted for range restriction. Even with this consideration in mind, the statistically significant independent variables in this study appear to be only weakly related to achievement.

Degree of Regulation of Home Education by the State

The degree of state regulation of home education had no effect on students' basic battery test scores. States were categorized as having either low regulation, moderate regulation, or high regulation. Low regulation was defined as no state requirement on the part of the home school parents to initiate any contact with the state. Moderate regulation was defined as the state requiring home school parents to send to the state notification or achievement test scores and/or evaluation of the student's learning by a professional. High regulation was defined as the state requiring home school parents to send to the state notification or achievement test scores and/or evaluation by a professional and, in addition, having other requirements (e.g., curriculum approval by the state, teacher qualifications of parents, or home visits by state officials). There was no significant difference between students' scores in these three groups. There was, therefore, no evidence that increased regulation of home education would increase the learning of students taught at home.

Test Administrator and Test Scores

The category of who administered the achievement test had little effect, in terms of practical significance, on basic battery test scores. All four test-administrator groups had scores that were well above the national average. There was no significant difference in scores between students who were tested by public school teachers and students who were tested by their parents. Scores of students who were tested by their parents were statistically significantly higher than scores of those tested by private school teachers and by others, but the difference was, practically speaking, rather unimpressive; all three groups were at or above the 81st percentile.

Use of Computer for Education of the Child and Test Scores

The use of a computer in the education of these home educated students had, in most cases, no effect on academic achievement. The statistical analyses that were done were for reading, language, math, science, and social studies. The only subject for which there was a significant difference was reading; those using computers for their education scored higher (i.e., the 88%ile) than those not using computers (i.e., the 85%ile). Practically speaking, this is an insignificant difference.

Graduates of Home Education

Two hundred thirty-two students in these families had been home educated and had graduated from their secondary school academic studies (i.e., high school). These students were home schooled for an average of 7 years. Immediately after high school graduation from home education, 25% went to a four-year college on a full-time basis, 17% went into full-time employment, 12% went into part-time higher education and part-time employment, and 25% said that they did other things. A further analysis was done of these "other" activities.

Overall, it was found, about 57% of home education graduates went immediately on to some form of formal postsecondary education, another 8% pursued apprenticeships or more home study, and 19% went into employment without simultaneous formal studies. In 1993, 62% of high school graduates, nationwide, went on to college the following academic year (United States Department of Education, Office of Educational Research and Improvement, 1995, p. 2).

Another way to summarize what these graduates did soon after their secondary or high school years is to only consider those who went on to some form of postsecondary education, full-time or part-time, or into employment. This analysis did not include those who went into the military, religious missions, religious ministry, volunteer work, unemployment, *et cetera*. This analysis revealed that 69% of the home educated went on to postsecondary education and 31% into employment. For the same two categories for the general United States public, 71% go on to postsecondary education while 29% go into employment (United States Department of Education, Office of Educational Research and Improvement, 1996b, Table 2-6).

The findings of this study suggest that home school graduates pursue postsecondary studies at a rate similar to that for graduates of conventional schools. It is not known, however, at what rate the home educated complete high school studies; home education advocates say that it is a very high rate. In the general public, the dropout rate from high school is about 13% (United States Bureau of the Census, 1994a).

Longitudinal Findings

Families and children who were involved in both Ray's 1990 nationwide study and this study were compared with respect to several factors. It appears that the differences were minor with respect to most factors such as the father's education level, the mother's education level, family income, the cost per child to home educate, and the number of visits that families make to public libraries. One significant difference between these families compared to themselves several years apart was the average number of years that their children were home educated. In the first study, the average 3.1 and in this study it was 6.0. For these families, it appears that their plans to home educate their children through the 8th to 12th grade are being realized. If this trend continues and the home education population continues to grow at the rate of at least 15% annually (Ray, 1996 and estimates based on this study), there could likely be 3 to 4 million children home educated during the 2005-2006 academic year.

Some other general differences between Ray's 1990 families and the families in this study appear to emerge. About 58% of the families in the former study had computers in their homes; 86% of the families in this study had computers in their homes. Furthermore, 84% of the children in this study used computers for educational purposes. (Comparable data were not collected in the earlier study.)

Another difference between the earlier study's (Ray, 1990b) families and these families appears to be in the area of the curriculum used by families. There may be a significant difference in that a parent-designed curriculum was used 67% of the time in 1990 and 71% of the time in this study. It is possible that over time parents become more confident in their own abilities. It is also possible that the home education community has developed more resources to help parents design their own curricula. The greatest change was in the use of a complete curriculum package; it decreased from 31% in 1990 to 24% in this study. The choice options presented to parents, however, were slightly different in the two studies and the sample populations included in the two studies were possibly different.

Students who were involved in both studies maintained their relatively high academic achievement over the years. This is a significant finding and is consistent with other research that shows that long-term home education has a neutral to positive effect on children's academic performance (Ray, 1994, p. 53, 1995; Russell, 1994). These children's reading, listening, language, math, science, social studies, basic battery, and complete battery achievement test scores were analyzed. For each subject area and testing category, these students' scores were statistically the same in the two studies. In both studies, the scores were well above the national average of conventional school students.

As was noted earlier, there are always limitations to research such as this which involves *ex post facto* comparisons. Wright (1988) suggested that various statistical techniques be employed to compare home education students to those in public and private schools. Some studies (e.g., Russell, 1994; Ray, 1994; and this study) have used multivariate techniques to address some of these limitations. On another topic, increasing the response rate would enhance confidence that the sample was representative. It is generally recognized that volunteers tend to be better educated and have higher social-class status than nonvolunteers (Borg & Gall, 1989, p. 228). The findings from the volunteers in this study, however, are consistent with many other studies that had both higher and lower response rates. This is evidence, then, that these findings are valid. Wright (1988) and others (Cizek, 1993; Ray, 1988) have also suggested that studies should attempt to broaden the areas of evaluation (e.g., critical thinking and motivational attitudes). Future researchers might do well to continue to consider such suggestions. Despite these limitations, the author will proceed with some interpretive commentary.

Strengths of Home Education

The findings of this study and the growing body of research lead me to many inferences—several of these are related to the strengths of home education families. Here I present some of those strengths.

Parents Choose to Build Strong Families

The first strength is that parents can — and do — choose to construct and maintain strong, stable families that provide a nourishing home education environment for their children's learning and social development. Evidence for this comes in several forms.

One form of evidence is that these children show strikingly strong academic performance and they are apparently healthy in terms of social and psychological development (Numerous references have already been provided in this report.) Some researchers (e.g., Delahooke, 1986; Shyers, 1992) have posited that that these children's increased interaction time with adults, as compared to time with peers, is contributing to their social and psychological health. Not only does descriptive research show that they have high academic performance at given points in time, but research also supports the idea that long-term home schooling either maintains or improves the strong achievement over time. Studies indicate that these children are involved in a moderate amount of social interaction. They interact with a variety of people outside of the family in a variety of contexts. This activity outside of the family, however, is at a level that still allows them a relatively large amount of time to be with and learn from their parents compared to children who are with peers and non-family members in conventional schools for a large portion of their everyday lives.

Perhaps significantly, this relatively large amount of time with "family members" involves parents who are a married man and woman. It has become clear that all but a few home schooling families are guided by a married husband and wife. As sociologists and family experts testify, this is a clearly significant factor in late 20th-century America. The simple fact that essentially all of these home educated children have a "good family man" (Blankenhorn, 1995, p. 208) and a mother leading their families suggests that they, on average, have an advantage over many other children in America. Actually, the simple fact that they *have a father at all* is evidence that they are at an advantage compared to a quickly growing portion of children in America (Popenoe, 1996, p. 191). Blankenhorn conducted focus groups with a broad cross-section of married, middle-class America and, based on their ideas, defined the "good family man." He is a man who is a provider and protector, shows love for his wife and children through his actions, has biblical and moral values, and is flexible as a partner with his spouse (Blankenhorn, 1995, p. 208). It should be pointed out that Blankenhorn's subjects, who defined the "good family man," spoke of biblical and moral values even though they were not all of Judeo-Christian faiths. That is, a good family man possesses these traits regardless of his religious affiliation. It appears, from the research on home education to date, that fathers who home educate their children are generally "good family men."

In addition, the time that these children have with their family involves a parent, usually the mother, who stays at home to raise, train, and educate them. This mother and her husband keep alive and robust the "traditional" things that families have done. People such as Martin (1992), however, claim that families no longer do— nor will do—these traditional things so that schools, as "schoolhomes," must do them. This home schooling father and mother vitalize the type of home and family that provide the basics of care, concern, and connection that Martin says conventional schools, as moral equivalents of the home, must increasingly provide. These home schooling families provide food, shelter, clothing, education, and significant doses of social capital (Coleman & Hoffer, 1987; Ray, 1989), including care, concern, and connection. It could be argued that even conventional schools that are specifically designed (by educational and social planners such as Martin) to provide care, concern, and connection do not provide as much of these intangibles as does a family of very modest means that is headed by a husband and his wife.

Along the same lines, it should be noted that the preceding discussion of husband-wife families should *not* be construed as claiming that single parents should not, cannot, nor do not (successfully) home educate children. In fact, many single parents are successfully doing so. It is often difficult for single parents to home school, however, because of the increased demands on their time and energy that may accompany home schooling.

Parents Take Primary Responsibility—and Participate in Their Villages

The second strength is that these parents accept and fulfill their responsibility to *personally* raise and educate their children. That is, they do not excessively depend on their villages, their communities and the state, to raise and educate their children.

The contemporary thinking of many in positions of leadership and academe is that, to use an old African proverb, "it takes a village to raise a child." State (public) schools are often promoted as the key actor in the villages. For example, the theme for the American Educational Research Association's (AERA) 1995 annual meeting was "partnerships for a new America" (AERA, 1995). At the meeting, many professional educators, mainly academics, promoted the concept that state schools must become sites of comprehensive social, psychological, and physical health services for children (AERA, 1995, e.g., sessions 50.61 & 56.12). According to these people, the village is, presumably, a collaboration of all the different segments of society gathering around an innocent baby to protect him, to teach him, and to love him (James, 1996). These segments of society would include institutions and groups such as state social services, state schools, government-run libraries, boys and girls clubs, nurseries and daycares, neighbors, churches, friends, and family (by marriage, birth, and adoption).

Some writers (e.g., Clinton, 1996) offer limited obligatory praise to the traditional two-parent family with one parent who serves as a homemaker. At the same time, these authors argue for notable increases in state and federal services for raising children. They tend to claim that things are different now from the 1950s, when this particular type of traditional family was the norm, and that today's society must adjust (Clinton, 1996; Martin; 1992). They present a presumed pragmatic philosophy and methodology to develop an ever-increasing role for the government in raising children.

For example, Clinton (1996) fondly reminisces about her childhood in the 1950s and how her parents and the parents in her neighborhood provided great security for her and other children. She explains that things are different now because more mothers are leaving the home to work while in the 1950s mothers were staying at home to raise their children. However, rather than using concrete evidence to address whether stay-at-home mothers (or fathers) are a psychological, educational, and social benefit to children, Clinton (1996) (and others, e.g., Martin, 1992) appear to unquestioningly accept the practice of two parents working outside the home and having others raising their children. In addition, such authors may make an anecdotal or emotional appeal that introduces doubt regarding whether the "good traditional family" of the 1950s was really good after all (e.g., Clinton, 1996, p. 29). (Blankenhorn, 1995, documents that this is a common and popular practice of academics and cultural leaders who are denying the importance of the traditional family and fathers.)

The solution for these thinkers is a significantly increased role for government agencies and state social workers and an increase in tax-subsidized "private" childcare and educational services (Buehrer, 1995; Clinton, 1996, p. 136-141, 207-213, 221; Duffy, 1995; Martin, 1992). Interestingly, there is no vigorous effort by these people to promote thinking and social policy that would actively encourage and support parents to decide to be full-time homemakers and parents.

My appraisal is that those who call for more tax-funded and state-run services, programs, and controls may be guilty of the is-ought fallacy. More parents leaving their children more often and for more time may not be the best for children and their learning and development. On the contrary, the empirical evidence "... shows that by far the best environment for childrearing is in the home and under the care of the biological parents. The more both parents can be in close contact with the child in the early years, the better. It also indicates that every infant needs one special person to whom he or she can become attached, a person who cares about the child beyond reason. That person typically has been the biological mother, the person most highly motivated for the task" (Popenoe, 1996, p. 214). More of the nation's leaders and academics should carefully consider the evidence before proposing policy and quiescently accepting *what is*—the demographic trends of the day.

In addition, one could argue, along with James (1996), an African American, that three fundamental problems arise with the use of the old African proverb that says, "It takes a village to raise a child." "First, children do not belong to the *village* or to the community or to the government. They belong to parents and the *village* exists as a resource for these families. Second, even if we did believe this to be true, the *village* no longer exists" (James, 1996, p. 1). Third, James argues, those who are planning for the *village* to raise children are, in many ways, simply building a larger government that cannot be successful in raising children. Along these lines, it is clear from the research base that home educators have decided to take upon themselves the raising and educating of their children and not look to a *village* to do it for them. They appear to agree with writers who argue that the best approach to raising well-educated and psychologically-healthy children is to do so with minimal involvement with state-controlled programs (e.g., Buehrer, 1995; Duffy, 1995; Richman, 1994).

Home education parents have, by definition, accepted the primary responsibility for the education and training of and provision for their offspring. Simultaneously, however, these parents do value and participate with a variety of people, organizations, and institutions throughout their communities, their states, and across their nation (Lines, 1996; see also findings in this report). They have neither rejected their villages nor have they turned over their children to be raised by their villages. Home educators and their families show ". . . an interest in participating in the life of a community wider than a family" (Lines, 1994, p. 20), are socially active (Mayberry, Knowles, Ray, & Marlow, 1995), and the content of their magazines (e.g., *Growing Without Schooling, The Home School Court Report*, and *The Teaching Home*) show that they are very interested in the political life of their local communities, states, and country. That is to say, they have a strong dedication to their families but they are, by and large, socially engaged.

These parents and their children are active in their churches and synagogues, political and civic groups, home education organizations, and a multitude of community activities such as athletic teams, 4H, and scouts. As Lines (1994, p. 21) explained,

". . . these homeschoolers are asserting their historic individual rights so that they may form more meaningful bonds with family and community. In doing so, they are not abdicating from the American agreement. To the contrary, they are affirming it." It appears that these parents are — and are teaching their children to be — proactively engaged in society.

The Home Education Environment is Linked to High Academic Achievement

The third strength is that the practice of home education is positively related to students' academic achievement, learning ability, and thinking skills. This strength was alluded to earlier in this section. Although America's conventional schools have taken on an increasing number of social and psychological roles during the past century, the enhancement of academic achievement, literacy, and thinking abilities are still supposed to be the primary purpose of schools. Findings made in this study and many others substantiate that home educated students perform well in terms of academics and thinking skills. (Numerous references have already been provided in this report.) Despite the limitations of research on these children's learning (Lines, 1996, p. 66; Wright, 1988), research findings at least hint that there may be a causal link between home education and positive academic performance and thinking skills.

Multivariate analyses of various demographic and other significant factors that often explain variance in children's learning are instructive. They show that numerous background variables which are important in the public school setting have relatively little importance within the home education environment. Some of these variables are the formal teacher-training of parents, family income, and formal educational attainment of the parents. (This specific phenomenon is addressed later as another strength.) In addition, research has provided some evidence that the longer students are home educated, the better they perform in terms of academic achievement; at minimum, they maintain their high performance. One might ask: Why do the home educated have high academic achievement even when various indicators might predict that a particular family's children would not do well?

The apparently simple learning environment that is found in home education may, in reality, be too complex to reduce to its salient and critical elements with regard to what makes it an effective educational environment. Books and journal articles abound on the topic of effective schools (e.g., Stockard & Mayberry, 1992). In general, research and opinion on this topic is about conventional schools. Research has shown that schools help students learn when schools value the teaching of academic subjects and hold high expectations for students; someone (e.g., the principal) is an instructional leader; the students find themselves in an orderly and pleasant atmosphere; there is significant feedback to and individualization for students; and students and teachers have positive feelings about their environment and have high morale (Good & Brophy, 1987, p. 152-153, 204, 251, 390-391; Stockard & Mayberry, 1992, p. 34-35).

Findings such as those just mentioned regarding conventional classroom schools may apply, to varying degrees, to home education. For example, researchers have found that two of parents' main reasons for home schooling are to emphasize academics and to provide an orderly and moral social environment for their children that is consistent with the parents' values (Batterbee, 1992; Ray, 1992b, 1993). In addition, I am meeting an increasing number of home education leaders who say that the parents are seeking physical safety for their children via home schooling. Perhaps home educators are succeeding in these areas. Are there, however, other elements that make home education successful?

I would like to suggest four elements that might explain the apparent learning success of the home educated and the lack of practically significant relationships between these students' academic achievement and the independent variables examined in this study and in other studies. These elements may be interrelated.

Value Consistency, Value Communities, and Social Capital

First, and perhaps most importantly, home schooling families presumably possess a large measure of social capital (Coleman & Hoffer, 1987). Social capital ". . . exists in the *relations* between persons" (Coleman & Hoffer, p. 221). Coleman and Hoffer presented trust as a form of social capital. "A group within which there is extensive trustworthiness and extensive trust is able to accomplish much more than a comparable group without that trustworthiness and trust" (Coleman & Hoffer, p. 221). They gave evidence that even if families possess high levels of human capital (i.e., skills and capacities in people as may be acquired in schools), the children may be at an academic disadvantage if there is little social capital in the family. This low level of social capital might be caused by the physical absence of family members (i.e., a "structural deficiency") or the absence of strong relations between children and parents (i.e., a "functional deficiency"). Coleman and Hoffer used the construct of social capital to explain why private school students outperform public school students in terms of academic achievement. I have used Coleman and Hoffer's work to present a modest model—the educational resource niche—and accompanying theoretical comments (Ray, 1989, 1990c).

The educational resource niche includes the dimensions of physical capital, human capital, and social capital and uses them to describe children's learning environments and, perhaps, to predict academic achievement. With respect to science learning, I posited that this three-dimensional model could help explain why specific students achieve well even if their parents are not professionally trained teachers, have relatively low levels of income, and lack resources at home such as computers and sophisticated laboratory equipment (Ray, 1989, p. 9-10). The concept that social capital is relatively more important than either human or physical capital could be applied to successful learning in any subject matter in the home education environment.

As a part of their overall analysis that hinges on social capital, Coleman and Hoffer (1987) discussed the importance of value consistency and value communities. That is, the sharing of values between school personnel, parents, and students leads to efficient social function and schools in which students learn effectively. My view is that the home education environment and home education communities appear to provide a high level of value consistency and a shared-value community in which children may successfully learn. Children who engage in home-based education are presented by their parents, friends, home education communities, and religious groups with a relatively coherent worldview—rather than the menagerie of competing value systems that is often encountered in state schools. Students whose learning is based in the home experience a safe and relatively orderly daily environment—rather than an environment that includes frequent threats to personal beliefs, threats to physical safety, geographic displacement (via busing or long commutes out of the neighborhood), and unnecessary separation from close family members. In sum, research and other evidence suggest to me that home education typically provides an emotionally warm, physically safe, academically challenging, and philosophically consistent place in which to learn.

Tutoring

A second element that might explain home educated students' academic success is tutoring. Many home educated children are essentially tutored. That is, they have private instructors, their parents, in a one-to-one or small group instructional setting. The average home schooling family has about three children. One of these is preschool age and two are in the conventional grades K-to-12 range. Thus, there is one adult teaching only two children most of the day. When the other parent is not at work, there are potentially two adults to teach two children. Even when the family is larger, for example with six children, the parent who teaches most of the academics is still only teaching five children. In these larger families, furthermore, it is often the case that the older children help teach the younger ones. Again, then, this approaches a one-to-one tutoring situation.

Literature on tutoring defines it and explains its advantages. For example, Bloom (1984, p. 4) explained that, in tutoring, "Students learn the subject matter with a good tutor for each student, or for two or three students simultaneously. This tutoring instruction is followed periodically by formative tests, feedback-corrective procedures, and parallel formative tests as in the mastery learning classes. The need for corrective work under tutoring is very small." Bloom and his associates tried to find teaching-learning methods that were as effective as tutoring. Bloom (1984, p. 6) stated, regarding some controlled research settings, that ". . . the most striking of the findings is that under the best learning conditions we can devise—(tutoring)—the average student is 2 sigmas [2 standard deviations of the control group] above the average control student taught under conventional group methods of instruction." In the home education setting, qualitative researchers have witnessed ongoing feedback, formative evaluation, intimate interaction during academic learning, and efforts by parents to holistically affect every area of their children's lives (e.g., Taylor, 1993, p. 85, p.133; Treat, 1990, p. vii, 120-136). These findings, and those on academic achievement, suggest that the practices and benefits of tutoring may be intrinsic in home schooling.

The preceding comments about tutoring enlisted the language of modern professional educators. A more historical and perhaps more accessible approach (Gordon & Gordon, 1990), however, may be more useful to this discussion. In their book *Centuries of Tutoring*, Gordon and Gordon (1990, p. 6) said: "Tutoring, as we will use it, encompasses the academic, moral and philosophical growth of the individual child. Tutors identified themselves closely with their pupils." Tutors often became quasi-family members and tutoring made education a family affair.

It often involved the parents with the tutor in combining education and the family as a unified life-long experience. This is what distinguished a "tutor" from a "classroom teacher." The tutor's highly individualistic approach transcended education's academic lessons. At its best tutoring attempted to reach out and touch a child's intellectual, moral and spiritual fiber in a dynamic personal process. The tutor remained a counselor into adulthood, long after the lessons had ceased. These concepts were found originally in the "tutorial ideal" of the ancient world. (Gordon & Gordon, p. 6)

There is great potential for individualization and flexibility in pedagogy, for mastery learning, and for the development of close and loving relationships between pupil and teacher in the tutorial method. Further research may document that these aspects of tutoring are commonplace amongst home education families. In connection with this, and as mentioned earlier in a different context, numerous examinations of effective educational environments by observers who hold very different worldviews have explained the benefits of such characteristics (e.g., Bloom, 1984; Coleman & Hoffer, 1987; Good & Brophy, 1987, especially chapters 9 & 11; Martin, 1992; Nash, 1990; Stockard & Mayberry, 1992). In the estimation of Good and Brophy (1987, p. 352), experts in the field of effective schools and instruction, private individualized tutoring ". . . is the method of choice for most educational purposes, because both curriculum (what is taught) and instruction (how it is taught) can be individualized and because the teacher can provide the student with sustained personalized attention . . ." Good and Brophy went on to say: "Unfortunately, private tutoring is too expensive for most families to afford" (p. 352). They might have spoken too soon on this matter or were not aware of or chose to ignore the growing home education movement when they wrote their book in the mid-1980s. Home educators have found that tutoring is very affordable if the tutor is the parent. Home educators have shown, furthermore, that tutoring by parents who are not professionally trained educators is very effective.

Academic Learning Time

The third element is that students at home may experience more academic learning time (ALT) (or academic engaged time,

AET) than do students in conventional schools. ALT is ". . . the amount of time a student spends performing relevant academic tasks with a high level of success . . ." (Good & Brophy, 1987, p. 35). High ALT is generally associated with high academic achievement. Data show that home educated students spend only 3 to 4 hours per day in structured learning compared to the 6 or more hours per day in school plus homework that conventional school students experience. The relatively small amount of time that the home educated spend in academics may be, in fact, largely ALT. One researcher (Duvall, 1994) has already found evidence of this in the home schooling setting.

Social Interaction and Distraction

Finally, the fourth element that might explain the high academic achievement of the home educated deals with social interaction. To put it simply, the home educated do not have to deal with the constant distractions that are attendant to a peer group. In a conventional school, students are constantly surrounded by the verbal and nonverbal behavior of their peers who are, psychologically and socially, very important to them. I recognize that peer pressure can be positive and motivate students to higher achievement and better behavior. In many instances, however, peer pressure distracts students from academic pursuits, reduces their efficient use of time, and draws students into behaviors that are neither beneficial nor virtuous (Coleman, 1961 [cited in Smith, 1992]; Smith, 1992; Larson, 1983 [cited in Smith, 1992]). Many parents recognize this social problem.

The verbal and nonverbal behavior that permeates a conventional school is usually that which many adults consider "normal" and relatively harmless. There is, however, another well-documented realm of behavior by which conventional school students are distracted—violence. For example, the United States Department of Justice's 1991 *National Crime Survey* reported that almost 3 million violent crimes and thefts were occurring on public school campuses annually (National School Safety Center News

Service, 1991 [cited in Klicka, 1993]). Toch (1991a, p. 66) reported that the exodus from public schools was largely fueled by the fact that, "Many parents view the public schools as ineffective and dangerous, and are exploring other options before it's too late." Few, if any, would argue that exposure to violence is the proper way to help children excel in academics.

Parents consistently explain that one of their main reasons for home educating their children is to positively and proactively govern the social interactions and moral development of their children (Mayberry, Knowles, Ray, & Marlow, 1995; Ray, 1992b; Van Galen, 1988). It may be that a side effect of this desire and action to help their children in terms of social and moral development is to free their children to spend more productive time on academics. If this is the case, then their academic achievement, naturally, would be enhanced.

In spite of the fact that various professional educators (e.g., National Association of Elementary School Principals, 1989-1990, p. 4; National Association of State Boards of Education, 1993; National Education Association, 1990) claim that home education is bad for children, research evidence continues to mount that home education benefits children. It may simply be that the advantages that were explained above outweigh the potential advantages of state schools. The conjectural advantages of state schools are things such as professionally trained and state-certified teachers; experiencing an ostensibly wide variety of cultures and worldviews; academic and extracurricular activities that may not be available to the home educated; a quality and quantity of laboratory and technical equipment that exceeds what most families possess; school personnel who are supposed to be receptive to and tolerant of a variety of philosophical and religious beliefs and the expression thereof; 6 to 9 hours of daily social interaction with a large number of same-age peers; and 6 to 9 hours with a variety of adults outside of the family who are, generally, not psychologically close to the child. The weight of research evidence, however, suggests that the lack of these things that are claimed to be advantages is not harming the home educated.

In summary, the various studies related to the learning and thinking skills of home educated students, almost without exception, lead to the conclusion that a variety of families who represent a varied philosophical and religious worldviews, socioeconomic statuses, and races and ethnicities are clearly successful at teaching their children via home education. Regarding the cause of these children's high academic achievement, however, there is little consensus and the problem has not been thoroughly investigated.

Home Education May Ameliorate the Negative Effects of Background Variables on Students' Achievement

The fourth strength is that home education may be conducive to eliminating the potential negative effects of certain background factors. Low family income, low parental educational attainment, parents not having formal training as teachers, race or ethnicity of the student, gender of the student, not having a computer in the home, infrequent usage of public services (e.g., public libraries), a child commencing formal education relatively later in life, relatively small amounts of time spent in formal educational activities, and a child having a large (or small) number of siblings seem to have little influence on the academic achievement of the home educated. (Several references were provided earlier.)

More specifically, in home education, educational attainment of parents, gender of student, and income of family may have weaker relationships to academic achievement than they do in public schools. This study found a few weak relationships between certain background variables and achievement. I have pointed out before, ". . . the strength of the relationships . . . are not unusual when one considers other research on academic achievement (Coleman, Hoffer, & Kilgore, 1982, p. 143-146; Snow, Barnes, Chandler, Goodman, & Hemphill, 1991)" (Ray, 1992, p. 32 a). In 1994, I repeated the idea that home education appears to ameliorate the effect of background variables (Ray, 1994). This is consistent with Coleman, Hoffer, and Kilgore's (1982, p. 144) conclusion that:

The first and most striking result is the greater homogeneity of achievement of students with different parental education levels in Catholic schools than in public schools. . . . . . That is, the performance of children from parents with differing educational levels is more similar in Catholic schools than in public schools (as well as being, in general, higher) . . . . Thus we have the paradoxical result that the Catholic schools come closer to the American ideal of the "common school," educating all alike, than do the public schools. Furthermore, . . . a similar result holds for race and ethnicity.

As I have suggested before (Ray, 1992a, 1994), it is likely that certain statistically significant variables in this study—father's education level, mother's education level, and gender of the student—explain less variance in student achievement in the home education setting than in the conventional classroom setting. It would be fascinating to see someone carefully and rigorously explore this hypothesis.

Home Education Builds Up Society

The fifth strength is that home education families individually, and the home education movement in general, appear to support and build up society rather than act as a burden upon society. Taxpayers do not have to spend, on home educated children, the nearly $6,000 of direct costs that is annually spent per student in public schools. This would have amounted to $3.7 to $6.1 billion during the 1996-1997 academic year if there were 700,000 to 1.15 million students home educated that year (Ray, 1996). In addition, taxpayers do not have to spend the extra large sums of money that state schools would have to use for construction, equipment and debt financing were the hundreds of thousands of home educated students in public schools.

The home education families appear to be efficient as they spend only $550 per child per year for home education. They are succeeding at educating their children to be competent in literacy, arithmetic, and thinking skills while using this modest sum of money that comes from their private, family resources. These children, who are taught by their parents and whose education is financed by their parents, are high academic achievers and healthy in terms of social and psychological development. Finally, these parents appear to be dedicated to the practice of long-term home education while not asking for much, if anything, from the state in order to teach their own children (Farris, 1990; Mayberry, Knowles, Ray, & Marlow, 1995, ch. 5).

Parents and Their Children Do Well With Minimal State Regulation

The sixth strength is that home education parents and their children perform well with minimal state regulation. This is indicated by the findings, of this study and of others, on children's academic achievement and social and psychological development.

States vary widely regarding the degree to which they regulate, via statutes and rules, home educators and their families (Klicka, 1996). Some states focus on the background traits of parents. For example, North Dakota requires that a parent be a certified teacher, have a baccalaureate degree, have a GED certificate and be monitored by a state-certified teacher, or meet a cut-off score on a national teacher exam. Some states require students to be given, annually, standardized achievement tests. In some states, home schools operate as private or church schools. In other states, the regulations are almost nonexistent. For example, in Idaho the home educated must simply be "otherwise comparably instructed" (as compared to education in conventional schools), with no approval involved (Klicka, 1996, p. 15). Data show that regardless of the degree of state regulation, the home educated students perform well in terms of academic achievement. (See the results of this study; see Ray, 1990b; see also a variety of state-specific studies mentioned earlier in this report and in Ray, 1992b). That is to say, there is no evidence that maintaining or increasing the degree of state regulation of home education will enhance children's learning.

The Home Educated Succeed in Adulthood

Finally, the seventh strength is that home education appears to prepare students to be successful and productive adults. For instance, a significant portion of home educated young adults go on to postsecondary educational pursuits, as data in this study and others indicate. There is also evidence that they succeed in colleges and universities (Galloway & Sutton, 1995; Oliveira, Watson, & Sutton, 1994). In fact, several colleges are now actively recruiting home educated students (e.g., personal communication, Bob Jones, June 3-7, 1991; personal communication, Lincoln Tamayo, November 28, 1990; personal communication, Miguel Sanchez, April 1996). Furthermore, many home educated adults are successful at obtaining gainful employment, they are not a financial burden on society, and they think well of having been home educated (Knowles & Muchmore, 1995).

Closing Remarks

This study expands the body of research on home education. It gives us more knowledge and insight regarding this resurgent educational practice. Future research will do even more to tell us about home education and its impact on individuals, families, and society. More importantly, however, the lives of the home educated in decades to come and the heritage that they bequeath to their children may inscribe a sweeping, indelible, and immeasurable mark on the history of 21st-century America.

Appendices

Appendix A

The normal curve with percentile equivalents.

From Hopkins, Kenneth D., Glass, Gene V., & Hopkins, B.R.
Basic statistics for the behavioral sciences, 2nd edition, p. 52.
Copyright © 1987 by Allyn and Bacon (originally Prentice-Hall).
Reprinted/adapted by permission.

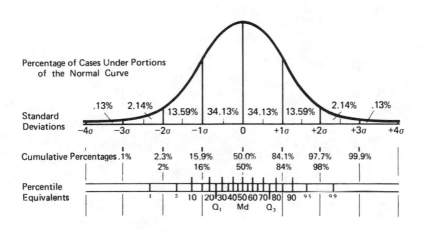

Appendix B

Questionnaire Instrument

Part A. INFORMATION REGARDING THE PARENTS AND FAMILY

Note: Any time you want to specify "Father" or "Mother" in your response, please use "F" for Father and "M" for Mother. Please answer all questions as for the 1994-1995 school year, unless otherwise noted.

1. How many years of formal schooling did each parent have? (e.g., completed high school = 12; bachelor's degree = 16; master's = 18; doctorate = 22) _____Father _____Mother

2. What percentage of the formal academic teaching is done by each parent? (Total should equal 100.)
_____ Father _____ Mother _____ Other situation

3. Has the **Father** ever been a state-certified teacher?
_____ Yes _____ No
    4. Is his certification current? ___ Yes ___ No
    5. Is/was the father's certification from the state in which he is currently living? ___ Yes _____ No

6. Has the **Mother** ever been a state-certified teacher?
_____ Yes _____ No
    7. Is her certification current? ___ Yes ___ No
    8. Is/was the mother's certification from the state in which she is currently living? ___ Yes _____ No

9. Does your family get a newspaper regularly? ___Yes ___No

10. Does your family get any magazines regularly? ___Yes ___No

11. Are you on the membership or mailing list of any home education organization (i.e., local support group, statewide organization, or national organization)? ___Yes ___No

12. Do you subscribe to any home education periodical publication (e.g., newsletter, magazine)? ___Yes ___No

13. What are the parents' primary occupations, professions, or trades? Please select the **one category** that best represents each parent. F=Father, M=Mother. Use "other" only if you can't decide.

(1)___ Farmer, Farm Manager
(2)___ Homemaker, Home Educator
(3)___ Laborer (such as construction worker, car washer, farm worker)
(4)___ Manager (such as sales manager, office manager, school administrator, retail buyer)
(5)___ Military (such as career officer or enlisted person in the Armed Forces)
(6)_____ Office Worker (such as data entry clerk, bank teller, bookkeeper, secretary, mail carrier)
(7)_____ Operator of machines (such as meat cutter, assembler, welder, taxicab/bus/truck driver)
(8)___ Owner of a small business or restaurant, contractor
(9)_____ Professional such as accountant, registered nurse, engineer, banker, librarian, writer, social worker, actor, athlete, artist, politician, but not including school teacher

(10)_____ Professional such as minister, dentist, doctor, lawyer, scientist, college teacher
(11)_____ Protective Service (such as police officer, firefighter, detective, sheriff, security guard)
(12)_____ Sales (such as sales representative, advertising or insurance agent, real estate broker)
(13)_____ School Teacher such as elementary, junior high, or high school, but not college
(14)_____ Service Worker (such as hair stylist, practical nurse, child care worker, waiter, domestic, janitor)
(15)___ Technical (such as computer programmer, medical or dental technician, draftsperson)
(16)_____ Tradesperson (such as baker, auto mechanic, housepainter, plumber, phone/cable installer, carpenter)
(17)___ Other

14. What are your racial/ethnic backgrounds (F=Father, M=Mother)?

Father Mother
(1) ____ ____ White, not of Hispanic origin
(2) ____ ____ Black, not of Hispanic origin
(3) ____ ____ Hispanic, regardless of race
(4) ____ ____ Asian, Pacific Island, or Oriental
(5) ____ ____ American Indian or Alaskan Native
(6) ____ ____ Other (please specify): _____

15. Is the mother employed outside the home? ___ Yes ___ No
    16. If yes, indicate the **average** number of working **hours per week**: ____

17. How many children do you have? _____

18. $_____,000 was your total gross family annual income from all sources before taxes in 1994 (to the nearest thousand). (Give a range, for example $23,000 - $28,000, if you are not sure.)

19. ____% of income is from father. 20. ____% of income is from mother.

21. What is the geographical setting of your home? (1)___ Urban, central city
                                                     (2)___ Suburban, area surrounding a central city
                                                     (3)___ Rural, area outside of suburban and not central city

22. Is this a married-couple family? ___Yes ___No
23. Are you a single parent? ___ Yes ___ No
    24. If single, you are the: ___ Father ___ Mother
    25. If single, what is your marital status?
        (1)___ Single, never married   (3)___ Widowed
        (2)___ Divorced/separated   (4)___ Not married but living in marriage-like relationship

26. How would you categorize your religious preferences? Select the <u>one</u> that most accurately describes each parent's preference. Please indicate both parents: F=Father, M=Mother.

(1) ___ Adventist (Seventh-day)
(2) ___ Amish
(3) ___ Assembly of God
(4) ___ Baptist
(5) ___ Episcopal
(6) ___ Independent Charismatic
(7) ___ Independent Fundamental/Evangelical
(8) ___ Lutheran
(9) ___ Mennonite
(10) ___ Methodist
(11) ___ Nazarene
(12) ___ Pentecostal
(13) ___ Presbyterian
(14) ___ Reformed
(15) ___ Other Protestant
(16) ___ Catholic (Roman)
(17) ___ Eastern Orthodox
(18) ___ Other Christian
(19) ___ LDS (Latter-Day Saint, Mormon)
(20) ___ Jehovah's Witness
(21) ___ Jewish
(22) ___ Muslim
(23) ___ Buddhist
(24) ___ New Age
(25) ___ Other Eastern religion
(26) ___ Atheist
(27) ___ Other; please specify:_____

Would you describe yourselves as "born-again Christians"?
27. Father: ___ Yes ___ No   **28.** Mother ___ Yes ___ No

29 & 30. What is the response of your children's grandparents to your home schooling? (Check one per column.)

Paternal	**Maternal**	
(1)_____	(1)_____	Opposed
(2)_____	(2)_____	Opposed, but not interfering
(3)_____	(3)_____	Neutral
(4)_____	(4)_____	Originally opposed, now supportive
(5)_____	(5)_____	Supportive
(6)_____	(6)_____	Supportive and participating

31. ___ On average, how many times per <u>month</u> do your children go to the <u>public</u> library?

32. ___ How many times per <u>month</u> do your children go to <u>any</u> library (e.g., private and/or church and/or public)?

33. Do you have a computer of any kind in your home? ___Yes ___No
    34. If yes, do you use the computer for the home education of any of your children? ___Yes ___No

35. $_____ is the amount of money we spend, on the average, <u>per child per year</u> for home schooling. (Include tuition, textbooks, field trips, special resources, etc.)

36. To the best of your knowledge, did you participate in the nationwide study conducted by HSLDA and Dr. Ray and published in 1990? (One version is HSLDA's 8-page, green-covered booklet.) ___Yes ___No

Part B. INFORMATION CONCERNING YOUR LEGAL STATUS

Please answer the questions on this page as you would have at the <u>end of the 1994-1995 school year</u>.

1. ____ is the state in which you resided at the end of the 1994-95 school year. (Use the two-letter state abbreviation.)
2. Had you submitted any type of paperwork to the state or local school authorities to notify them of your home school by the end of the 1994-95 school year? ___Yes ___No

3. Which <u>one</u> of the following would have best described your legal status?
    (1) ___ We are underground.
    (2) ___ We have notified the district, but we are not attempting to fully comply with the state statute.
    (3) ___ We have satisfied the statutory requirements.
    (4) ___ We are in a current dispute concerning our home school's legal status.
    (5) ___ Other. Please Describe very briefly: _____

Answer the rest of the questions on this page according to your <u>current situation</u> (unless otherwise instructed).

4. Which kind of legal difficulties have you <u>ever</u> experienced. Please check all that apply:
    (1) ___ We have never had any legal difficulty.
    (2) ___ We have received negative correspondence from school officials.
    (3) ___ We have received negative phone calls from school officials.
    (4) ___ We have had school officials come to our home with regard to the legal status of our home school.
    (5) ___ We were required to appear before our school board for a hearing.
    (6) ___ We have been threatened with legal action by school officials.
    (7) ___ We have been threatened with legal action by lawyers from a government agency (prosecutors, etc.).
    (8) ___ We have had court actions filed against us.
    (9) ___ We have actually appeared in a court for a preliminary or brief hearing.
    (10) ___ We have had a full trial.
    (11) Do you have any comments? _____

5. Were you a member of the Home School Legal Defense Association (HSLDA) at the end of 1994-95? __Yes __No
6. Are you currently a member of HSLDA? ___Yes ___No

7. Have you ever called or written to <u>any</u> attorney (lawyer) for assistance regarding home education? ___Yes ___No If your answer is "no," please skip to the next section of the survey.
8. If the answer to #7 is yes, which of the following occurred? Please <u>check all that apply, but use only one column per item</u> (i.e., HSLDA <u>or</u> Other Lawyer, but not both):

HSLDA while members	Other Lawyer	
(1) ___	___	I asked for advice from a lawyer which required no follow up.
(2) ___	___	I asked for advice from a lawyer which required follow up.
(3) ___	___	Lawyer wrote back to me.
(4) ___	___	Lawyer called me back.
(5) ___	___	Lawyer wrote letter(s) to school officials on my behalf.
(6) ___	___	Lawyer made phone call(s) to school officials on my behalf.
(7) ___	___	Lawyer wrote letter(s) to prosecuting lawyers on my behalf.
(8) ___	___	Lawyer made phone call(s) to prosecuting lawyers on my behalf.
(9) ___	___	Lawyer assisted me with a school board appearance by submitting written paper work.
(10) ___	___	Lawyer supplied me with a lawyer for a school board hearing.
(11) ___	___	Lawyer filed an appeal of a school board decision in court or in an administrative agency.
(12) ___	___	After legal papers were filed against me by the government, lawyer got the charges dismissed.
(13) ___	___	Lawyer defended me in court for a truancy, child neglect, or other criminal charge.

Part C. INFORMATION REGARDING YOUR CHILDREN

It is important that you complete a <u>separate one of these forms (Part C) for each of your children</u>, even those who are no longer living in your home. Include children from a previous marriage **only** if you or your spouse are the primary custodial parent <u>and</u> the child is currently living in your home. **Answer the questions <u>as you would have at the end of June 1995</u>, unless otherwise instructed.** Please make extra copies of Part C if we haven't sent enough for one for each of your children.

1. Circle the number of this child (**1=oldest** of your children):   1   2   3   4   5   6   7   8   9   10
   Please answer the following questions concerning <u>this</u> child.
2. Age ____ (as of the end of June 1995)
3. ___Male   ___Female

4. What is this child's racial/ethnic background?
   (1)____ White, not of Hispanic origin
   (2)____ Black, not of Hispanic origin
   (3)____ Hispanic, regardless of race
   (4)____ Asian, Pacific Island, or Oriental
   (5)____ American Indian or Alaskan Native
   (6)____ Other (please specify): _____

5. ____ is the number of brothers and sisters that this child had at the end of June 1995. Please consider all siblings, including half- and step- and adoptive brothers and sisters, regardless of where they live.

●● **If this child was <u>under 5</u> as of the end of June 1995, answer <u>only</u> the next question (#6); otherwise, skip on to the following question. ●●**
6. Did you intend to home school this child when he or she reaches school age?
   ___Yes ___No (Skip this question if child was over 5 at the end of June.)

7. This child's Grade Level during the 1994-95 school year was ____.
8. Had this child ever been home schooled (as of June 1995)? ___Yes ___No If no, answer <u>only</u> the next question (#9).
9. Only for children **NEVER** home schooled as of June 1995. What type of school attended?
   (1)___ Public school exclusively
   (2)___ Private (independent) school exclusively
   (3)___ Attended both public and private (independent) school

●● **All remaining questions to be answered only for children who had <u>EVER</u> been home schooled as of June 1995. ●●**
Please answer the following questions concerning this child <u>for the 1994-1995 school year</u> (unless otherwise indicated).

10. Was this child being home schooled? ___Yes ___No

11. The **degree of structure** in the practice of home education varies greatly. It goes from a very unstructured (unschooling) learning approach, centered upon the child's present interests, to the use of a planned, structured, and highly prescribed curriculum. The method used for this child was (please circle response):
   Very <u>Unstructured</u> 1   2   3   4   5   6   7 Very Structured

12. ____hours per day: On average, how many <u>hours per day</u> was this child engaged in structured learning.

13. Consider **formal instruction** to be planned or intentional instruction in areas such as reading, writing, spelling, or arithmetic. It is done to meet a learning objective. Please complete this sentence: We began formal instruction of this child when he/she was the age of _____ (round to the nearest 1/2 year).

14. On average, how many <u>hours per week</u> was this child in **contact with other people?**
   (1)___ Adults outside the family, hours per week.
   (2)___ Siblings, hours per week (while awake).
   (3)___ Children outside the family, hours per week.

15. Check <u>all</u> of the following activities in which this child engaged during 1994-1995:

(1)___ Group sports (e.g., city, public school, church)
(2)___ Sunday school
(3)___ Bible clubs (e.g., Awana, Pioneer, Cadets)
(4)___ Field trips
(5)___ Volunteer work with people
(6)___ Music classes
(7)___ 4-H

(8) ___ Ballet/dance classes
(9) ___ Classes with students outside the home
(10)___ Scouts (e.g., Boy, Girl, Campfire)
(11)___ Play with people outside the family
(12)_____ Ministry (e.g., nursing home visits, prison ministry, child evangelism)
(13)___ Other (specify):_____

16. During a <u>typical month in 1994-1995</u>, how many times did this child do each of the activities below?

Activity	Never	Once	2-3 Times	4-7 Times	No Opportunity
(1) Attend church worship services	1	2	3	4	5
(2) Attend Sunday school classes	1	2	3	4	5
(3) Attend a church youth group	1	2	3	4	5

17 & 18. Please ask this <u>STUDENT to PERSONALLY respond to the next two questions</u>. If he is old enough to remember what he did during 1994-1995, please try to not influence his answers.

17. During last school year, how many hours a day did you USUALLY play video or computer games, such as Nintendo?

	On Weekdays (circle one)	On Weekend days (circle one)
Don't play video/computer games	1	1
Less than 1 hour a day	2	2
1 hour or more, less than 2	3	3
2 hours or more, less than 3	4	4
3 hours or more, less than 5	5	5
5 hours or more a day	6	6

18. During last school year, how many hours a day did you USUALLY watch TV or videotapes?

	On Weekdays (circle one)	On Weekend days (circle one)
Don't watch TV/Video	1	1
Less than 1 hour a day	2	2
1 hour or more, less than 2	3	3
2 hours or more, less than 3	4	4
3 hours or more, less than 5	5	5
5 hours or more a day	6	6

19. **Parent responds again:** What kind of curriculum did you use for this child during 1994-1995? (Mark <u>all</u> that apply.)

(1)____ Parent-designed curriculum (major components handpicked by parents)
(2)____ Satellite school curriculum
(3)____ Home school program provided by a local private school
(4)____ No particular curriculum plan
(5)____ Complete curricular package (includes language, social studies, mathematics, and science material for full year.) **20. If you check this option**, please indicate the ONE package you used for this child:

(1)___ A Beka, Pensacola FL
(2)___ Alaska State Dept. of Ed., Juneau AK
(3)___ Alpha Omega, Tempe AZ
(4)___ Basic Education (ACE), Dallas/Ft.Worth TX
(5)___ BJU Press, Greenville SC
(6)___ Calvert School, Baltimore MD
(7)___ Christian Liberty Acad., Arlington Hts. IL
(8)___ Christian Light, full service plan, Harrisb. VA
(9)___ Covenant Home Curriculum, Brookfield WI
(10)___ Evangelistic & Faith Enterpri. of Am., Oliver TN
(11)___ Hewitt Child Development Cntr, Washougal WA

(12)___ Home Study International, Takoma Park MD
(13)___ International Institute, Park Ridge IL
(14)___ Living Heritage Academy (See Basic Education)
(15)___ National Acad. Christian Ed., Reynoldsberg OH
(16)___ Oak Meadow Ed. Services, Blacksburg VA
(17)___ Our Lady of Victory, Mission Hills CA
(18)___ Seton School Home Study, Front Royal VA
(19)___ Summit Christian Academy, Dallas TX
(20)___ Sycamore Tree, Costa Mesa CA
(21)___ Other (Name/Location): _____

21. If you indicated a complete curricular package (#19), did you obtain it directly from the curriculum developer this year?
    (1)___ Yes, I obtained it during 1994-1995 from the developer.
    (2)___ No, purchased during an earlier year
    (3)___ No, purchased second hand
    (4)___ Other (please specify): _____

22. Was this child enrolled in any type of correspondence course, satellite school, local independent (private) school's home schooling program or the like? ___Yes   ___No

    23. If yes, please specify which program: _____
    24. This program is ___Local   ___National

25. The PRIMARY method of instruction used for this child in 1994-1995 was (choose only one):
    (1)___ ATI (Advanced Training Institute)
    (2)___ Classical Approach
    (3)___ Eclectic, directed by parent (i.e., mix of variety of methods with none dominant)
    (4)___ Principle Approach method
    (5)___ Traditional textbooks and assignments
    (6)___ Unit study method (e.g., KONOS, Weaver)
    (7)___ Unschooling, directed by child's choices and desires
    (8)___ Worktexts (e.g., ACE's PACEs, Christian Light Education)
    (9)___ Other (please specify): _____

26. Did you have a computer in your home that this child used for educational purposes? __Yes   __No
27. Had this child ever received special services as of the end of the 1994-1995 year for any special needs problems such as visual (not correctable by glasses), hearing, speech, orthopedic, physical disability, emotional, mental retardation, or special learning problems? ___Yes   ___No

Please answer the following concerning your child's educational history since turning age 5.
28. _____ is the number of years **taught at home** since reaching age 5.
29. _____ is the number of years attending **public school prior to home** schooling.
30. _____ is the number of years attending **private (independent) school prior to home** schooling.
31. _____ is the number of years attending **public school after home schooling.**
32. _____ is the number of years attending **private (independent) school after home** schooling.
33. _____ is the grade through which we intend to home school this child. (12=high school, 16=college)
34. This child ___was   ___was not home schooled during the 1994-1995 school year.

If this child was home schooled for the 1994-1995 school year, please answer the following questions regarding standardized achievement tests. (We know that #35 through #50 require much work on your part, but this is a very important part of this study.)

35. Has this child taken a standardized achievement test during the past 24 months? ___Yes ___No

Fill in all of the following that were reported for this child's **most recent achievement test** since June 1993:
36. Child took test during the ___1994-95 school year   ___1993-94 school year   ___this 1995-1996 school year

Please fill in any of the following which were reported for this child's test:

37. The name of the test this child took was:
    (1) ___ Iowa Test of Basic Skills (ITBS)
    (2) ___ Stanford Achievement Test (SAT, but not the SAT for college admission)
    (3) ___ California Achievement Test (CAT)
    (4) ___ Comprehensive Test of Basic Skills (CTBS)
    (5) ___ Metropolitan Achievement Test (MAT)
    (6) ___ Other (please specify name of test): _____

38. ____ was this child's age at the time of the testing.
39. ____ was the grade level of this test.

Please report this child's national percentile rank **scores. "National Percentile Rank" is usually noted as PR, National PR, or NPR on test result forms. They were as follow:**

40. ____ Total Reading
41. ____ Total Listening
42. ____ Total Language
43. ____ Total Math
44. ____ Science
45. ____ Social Studies

46. ____ Study Skills (or, work-study)
47. ____ Basic Battery total (or total battery; combination of reading, language, and math as reported by testing service)
48. ____ Complete Battery total (combination of all areas tested as reported by testing service)

49. **Please attach a copy of this child's test results** (if available) **to the last page of this Part C** section regarding him. Please black out your child's name and any other personal identification information. Write on the form the number of this child (1=oldest) as you indicated earlier in this Part C. Attach it at the end of this child's Part C forms.
____Yes, I have attached a copy of the test results. ____I **did not** attach a copy of test results.

50. Who administered the test?
(1)___ Public school teacher
(2)___ Private school teacher
(3)___ Parent
(4)___ Other (specify): _____

51-53. If this child has "graduated" from his/her high school-level studies, please answer #51-#53.
51. Immediately after high school "graduation," this child went to:
(1)___ Junior (or community) college full-time
(2)___ 4-year college full-time
(3)___ Trade school (e.g., welding, dental technician, cosmetology)
(4)___ Business school (e.g., secretarial, computers)
(5)___ Full-time employment
(6)___ Part-time employment
(7)___ Part-time higher education & part-time employment
(8)___ Military
(9)___ Other; please specify: _____

52. ____ is the number of years this child was home educated during his/her kindergarten through 12th grade years (and please round to the nearest 1/2 year).
53. May we have the name and address of this child, who is now an adult (if address is different from yours) in order to contact him/her for a future study of home-educated adults? (This information is optional, of course.)

(1) Last Name:_____

(2) First Name:_____

(3) Street Address: _____

(4) City:_____ (5) State:_____ (6) Zip Code:_____

54. **FOR EVERY CHILD of Yours.** This information will help with a future longitudinal study (see Part D).
In the spaces provided below, create an **anonymous ID number** for this child by writing:
A. Day of the month and year of the birthday of the student's **father**.
B. Day of the month and year of the birthday of the **student**.
C. Day of the month and year of the birthday of the student's **mother**.
Example: The father was born 2-04-54, the child on 10-15-78, and the mother was born on 5-20-57. (For the first of twins, end with 01, and for the second, 02.) Therefore, the child's code is **04-54-15-78-20-57-00.**

___ ___-___ ___-___ ___-___ ___-___ ___-___ ___-___ ___
Father   Child   Mother   Twins

Part D. LONGITUDINAL STUDY

A very important purpose of this study is to gather information on home education families over the past several years. In addition, the Home School Legal Defense Association (HSLDA) or the National Home Education Research Institute (NHERI) may want to do another longitudinal study in the future. We can learn many things that are helpful to home education by following families over time.

If you participated in the 1990 nationwide study sponsored by HSLDA, we strongly encourage you to at least provide, in Section D, your children's anonymous code numbers so that we can complete the longitudinal part of this study. And even if you did not participate in 1990, if you are willing to be contacted in the future in order that your children might be followed over time, please do the following:

1. Be sure that you complete the identification codes for each of the children you will include in Part C of this survey. The code we use will help keep the identity of your children anonymous.
2. Fill in your names and current address and phone numbers below.

Please **note**: This is not a required part of the survey. Your participation in this section, however, would greatly aid this study and future longitudinal research. The more who participate, the better the studies.

1. Parents' **Last** Name(s): _____

2. Parents' **First** Names: _____

3. Street Address: _____

4. City:_____ 5. State:_____ 6. Zip Code:_____

Phone Number(s): 7. home: (_____)_____ 8. work: (_____)_____

In summary, PLEASE BE SURE THAT YOU HAVE DONE THE FOLLOWING:

1. Completed parts A, B, and D regarding your family.
2. Completed a separate Part C **for each of your children**. We realize that this is time consuming, and we especially thank you for your great help in this part of the study.
3. Be sure that the test score forms that you have included have identifying marks (e.g., "Child No. 1," or "anonymous ID number" as described above) to link it with child 1, 2, 3, and so on.
4. Collate your forms and staple all of them together at the top left corner in this order: Part A, Part B, Part C for your first child with his test score form attached, Part C for second child, etcetera for the children, and finally Part D.

THANK YOU for your time, energy, and help in this important project that should benefit all home education families across the United States, and in other countries.

Please complete this survey (don't delay) and return it along with copies of achievement test results by December 11, 1995 to HSLDA. (If you miss this date, please send it as soon as possible thereafter.)

National Home Education Research Institute (NHERI)
5000 Deer Park Drive S.E.
Salem, Oregon 97301

phone (503) 375-7019

Appendix C

Detailed Statistical Data

Church-related activities of home educated children:

WORSHIP   Attend Church Worship Services, Monthly

Value Label	Value	Frequency	Percent	Valid Percent	Cum Percent
	0	131	3.7	3.7	3.7
Never	1	101	2.8	2.9	6.6
Once	2	271	7.6	7.7	14.3
4 to 7 Times	4	2985	83.3	85.0	99.4
No Opportunity	5	22	.6	.6	100.0
	.	72	2.0	Missing	
	Total	3582	100.0	100.0	

SSCLASS   Attend Sunday School Classes, Monthly

Value Label	Value	Frequency	Percent	Valid Percent	Cum Percent
	0	288	8.0	8.7	8.7
Never	1	155	4.3	4.7	13.3
Once	2	310	8.7	9.3	22.6
4 to 7 Times	4	2414	67.4	72.5	95.2
No Opportunity	5	161	4.5	4.8	100.0
	.	254	7.1	Missing	
	Total	3582	100.0	100.0	

YTHGRP   Attend Church Youth Group, Monthly

Value Label	Value	Frequency	Percent	Valid Percent	Cum Percent
	0	530	14.8	18.6	18.6
Never	1	427	11.9	15.0	33.5
Once	2	322	9.0	11.3	44.8
4 to 7 Times	4	1048	29.3	36.7	81.6
No Opportunity	5	526	14.7	18.4	100.0
	.	729	20.4	Missing	
	Total	3582	100.0	100.0	

One-sample t-tests comparing the home educated students' achievement test scores to the national average of the 50%ile (z-score = 0):

```
One Sample t-tests
```

Variable	Number of Cases	Mean	SD	SE of Mean
TOTRDG Total Reading	1594	1.1465	.840	.021

```
    Test Value = 0
```

Mean Difference	99% CI Lower	Upper	"	t-value	df	2-Tail Sig
1.15	1.092	1.201	"	54.51	1593	.000

Variable	Number of Cases	Mean	SD	SE of Mean
TOTLANG Total Language	1486	.8545	.895	.023

```
    Test Value = 0
```

Mean Difference	99% CI Lower	Upper	"	t-value	df	2-Tail Sig
.85	.795	.914	"	36.80	1485	.000

Variable	Number of Cases	Mean	SD	SE of Mean
TOTLIST Total Listening	580	1.0476	.849	.035

```
    Test Value = 0
```

Mean Difference	99% CI Lower	Upper	"	t-value	df	2-Tail Sig
1.05	.956	1.139	"	29.71	579	.000

```
One Sample t-tests
```

Variable		Number of Cases	Mean	SD	SE of Mean
TOTMATH	Total Math	1613	.9016	.874	.022

Test Value = 0

Mean Difference	99% CI Lower	Upper	"	t-value	df	2-Tail Sig
.90	.845	.958	"	41.41	1612	.000

Variable		Number of Cases	Mean	SD	SE of Mean
SCIENCE	Science	1133	1.0047	.824	.024

Test Value = 0

Mean Difference	99% CI Lower	Upper	"	t-value	df	2-Tail Sig
1.00	.942	1.068	"	41.05	1132	.000

Variable		Number of Cases	Mean	SD	SE of Mean
SOCSTUD	Social Studies	1099	1.0294	.820	.025

Test Value = 0

Mean Difference	99% CI Lower	Upper	"	t-value	df	2-Tail Sig
1.03	.966	1.093	"	41.61	1098	.000

One Sample t-tests

Variable	Number of Cases	Mean	SD	SE of Mean
STUDYSK Study Skills	916	.8694	.814	.027

Test Value = 0

Mean Difference	99% CI Lower	Upper	"	t-value	df	2-Tail Sig
.87	.800	.939	"	32.34	915	.000

Variable	Number of Cases	Mean	SD	SE of Mean
BASBATT Basic Battery	1338	1.0455	.810	.022

Test Value = 0

Mean Difference	99% CI Lower	Upper	"	t-value	df	2-Tail Sig
1.05	.988	1.103	"	47.21	1337	.000

Variable	Number of Cases	Mean	SD	SE of Mean
COMBATT Complete Battery	1092	1.1076	.797	.024

Test Value = 0

Mean Difference	99% CI Lower	Upper	"	t-value	df	2-Tail Sig
1.11	1.045	1.170	"	45.91	1091	.000

Comparing test scores by who administered the test:

```
- - - -  O N E W A Y  - - - - -


        Variable  BASBATT    Basic Battery
     By Variable  ADMTEST    Administrator Of Test

                              Analysis of Variance

                              Sum of        Mean          F      F
        Source        D.F.    Squares       Squares      Ratio  Prob.

Between Groups          3      15.3618       5.1206      7.9542  .0000
Within Groups        1258     809.8485       .6438
Total                1261     825.2103
```

```
                              Standard   Standard
Group         Count    Mean   Deviation   Error    95 Pct Conf Int for Mean

Grp 1          102    1.0478    .8388     .0831      .8831  TO   1.2126
Grp 2          171     .8709    .8605     .0658      .7410  TO   1.0008
Grp 3          526    1.1727    .7552     .0329     1.1080  TO   1.2374
Grp 4          463     .9849    .8238     .0383      .9096  TO   1.0601

Total         1262    1.0528    .8090     .0228     1.0081  TO   1.0975
```

```
GROUP        MINIMUM    MAXIMUM

Grp 1        -1.1800     2.3300
Grp 2        -1.6400     2.3300
Grp 3        -1.6400     2.3300
Grp 4        -1.5600     2.3300

TOTAL        -1.6400     2.3300
```

```
Levene Test for Homogeneity of Variances

    Statistic    df1     df2     2-tail Sig.
     2.8352       3      1258       .037
```

```
- - - - - O N E W A Y - - - - -
```

```
    Variable   BASBATT      Basic Battery
 By Variable   ADMTEST      Administrator Of Test
```

Multiple Range Tests: LSD test with significance level .05

The difference between two means is significant if
  MEAN(J)-MEAN(I) >= .5673 * RANGE * SQRT(1/N(I) + 1/N(J))
  with the following value(s) for RANGE: 2.77

    (*) Indicates significant differences which are shown in the lower
triangle

```
                              G G G G
                              r r r r
                              p p p p

                              2 4 1 3
        Mean      ADMTEST

         .8709    Grp 2
         .9849    Grp 4
        1.0478    Grp 1
        1.1727    Grp 3          * *
```

Grp 1 = public school teachers
Grp 2 = private school teachers
Grp 3 = parents
Grp 4 = others

Comparing test scores of students using a computer for education vs. those not using a computer for education:

t-tests for Independent Samples of CMPTRCHD   Computer Used For Educating Child

Variable	Number of Cases	Mean	SD	SE of Mean
TOTRDG Total Reading				
Ye	1119	1.1819	.839	.025
No	437	1.0594	.834	.040

      Mean Difference = .1225

Levene's Test for Equality of Variances: F= .002   P= .967

	t-test for Equality of Means				95%
Variances	t-value	df	2-Tail Sig	SE of Diff	CI for Diff
Equal	2.59	1554	.010	.047	(.030, .215)
Unequal	2.60	800.83	.009	.047	(.030, .215)

Variable	Number of Cases	Mean	SD	SE of Mean
TOTLANG Total Language				
Ye	1029	.8904	.898	.028
No	421	.7730	.886	.043

Mean Difference = .1174

Levene's Test for Equality of Variances: F= .041   P= .839

	t-test for Equality of Means				95%
Variances	t-value	df	2-Tail Sig	SE of Diff	CI for Diff
Equal	2.27	1448	.023	.052	(.016, .219)
Unequal	2.28	789.58	.023	.051	(.016, .218)

t-tests for Independent Samples of CMPTRCHD   Computer Used For Educating Child

Variable	Number of Cases	Mean	SD	SE of Mean
TOTMATH Total Math				
Ye	1126	.9196	.862	.026
No	447	.8554	.899	.043

Mean Difference = .0642

Levene's Test for Equality of Variances: F= .594   P= .441

```
       t-test for Equality of Means                                95%
Variances   t-value      df     2-Tail Sig    SE of Diff        CI for Diff
=============================================================================
Equal        1.32      1571        .188         .049         (-.031, .160)
Unequal      1.29     789.28       .197         .050         (-.033, .162)
=============================================================================
```

Variable	Number of Cases	Mean	SD	SE of Mean
SCIENCE Science				
Ye	787	1.0045	.811	.029
No	327	1.0014	.853	.047

Mean Difference = .0032

Levene's Test for Equality of Variances: F= 1.125 P= .289

```
       t-test for Equality of Means                                95%
Variances   t-value      df     2-Tail Sig    SE of Diff        CI for Diff
=============================================================================
Equal         .06      1112        .954         .054         (-.103, .110)
Unequal       .06     583.23       .954         .055         (-.105, .112)
=============================================================================
```

t-tests for Independent Samples of CMPTRCHD   Computer Used For Educating Child

Variable	Number of Cases	Mean	SD	SE of Mean
SOCSTUD Social Studies				
Ye	765	1.0311	.801	.029
No	316	1.0209	.867	.049

Mean Difference = .0103

Levene's Test for Equality of Variances: F= 1.033 P= .310

```
       t-test for Equality of Means                                95%
Variances   t-value      df     2-Tail Sig    SE of Diff        CI for Diff
=============================================================================
Equal         .19      1079        .852         .055         (-.097, .118)
Unequal       .18     547.72       .856         .057         (-.101, .122)
=============================================================================
```

Tables of correlation coefficients for all interval-data independent variables used in multiple regressions analyses in this study:

```
        - -  Correlation Coefficients   - -

           TOTRDG      TOTLANG      TOTMATH      COMBATT

FATHED      .1595       .2056        .1868        .2259
          ( 1550)     ( 1449)      ( 1566)      ( 1060)
          P= .000     P= .000      P= .000      P= .000

MOTHED      .1352       .1569        .1910        .1797
          ( 1568)     ( 1463)      ( 1586)      ( 1073)
          P= .000     P= .000      P= .000      P= .000

INCOME      .0828       .0875        .1032        .1020
          ( 1493)     ( 1393)      ( 1510)      ( 1023)
          P= .001     P= .001      P= .000      P= .001

COSTCHD     .0401       .0274        .0386        .0212
          ( 1523)     ( 1423)      ( 1541)      ( 1049)
          P= .118     P= .302      P= .130      P= .493

HOMEYRS     .0944       .0694        .0118        .0283
          ( 1568)     ( 1464)      ( 1588)      ( 1071)
          P= .000     P= .008      P= .640      P= .355

LIBRPUB     .0652       .0368        .0458        .0083
          ( 1434)     ( 1339)      ( 1449)      (  982)
          P= .014     P= .178      P= .081      P= .796

HRSSTRCT    .0012       .0405        .0487        .0202
          ( 1582)     ( 1476)      ( 1601)      ( 1083)
          P= .961     P= .120      P= .051      P= .507

AGEFORM    -.0660      -.0406       -.0606       -.0916
          ( 1574)     ( 1471)      ( 1594)      ( 1081)
          P= .009     P= .120      P= .015      P= .003
```

Key:
Coefficient
(Cases)
2-tailed Significance
" . " is printed if a coefficient cannot be computed.

Comparing achievement test scores across time for students who participated in both 1990 and 1996; t-tests for Paired Samples:

Variable	Number of pairs	Corr	2-tail Sig	Mean	SD	SE of Mean
TOTRDG Total Reading				1.2652	.742	.073
	102	.566	.000			
TOTRDG1				1.1442	.881	.087

Paired Differences			"			
Mean	SD	SE of Mean	"	t-value	df	2-tail Sig
.1210	.767	.076	"	1.59	101	.114
99% CI (-.078, .320)			"			

Variable	Number of pairs	Corr	2-tail Sig	Mean	SD	SE of Mean
TOTLIST Total Listening				.8469	.874	.219
	16	.553	.026			
TOTLIST1				1.0894	1.004	.251

Paired Differences			"			
Mean	SD	SE of Mean	"	t-value	df	2-tail Sig
-.2425	.896	.224	"	-1.08	15	.296
99% CI (-.902, .417)			"			

Variable	Number of pairs	Corr	2-tail Sig	Mean	SD	SE of Mean
TOTLANG Total Language				1.1596	.737	.087
	72	.682	.000			
TOTLANG1				1.0132	.844	.099

Paired Differences			"			
Mean	SD	SE of Mean	"	t-value	df	2-tail Sig
.1464	.638	.075	"	1.95	71	.055
99% CI (-.052, .345)			"			

t-tests for Paired Samples

Variable	Number of pairs	Corr	2-tail Sig	Mean	SD	SE of Mean
TOTMATH Total Math				.9322	.791	.078
	103	.461	.000			
TOTMATH1				.9615	.860	.085

Paired Differences			"				
Mean	SD	SE of Mean	"	t-value		df	2-tail Sig
-.0292	.859	.085	"	-.35		102	.731
99% CI (-.251, .193)			"				

	Number of		2-tail				
Variable	pairs	Corr	Sig		Mean	SD	SE of Mean
SCIENCE Science					1.1123	.858	.168
	26	.644	.000				
SCIENCE1					1.1977	.905	.177

Paired Differences			"				
Mean	SD	SE of Mean	"	t-value		df	2-tail Sig
-.0854	.745	.146	"	-.58		25	.564
99% CI (-.493, .322)			"				

	Number of		2-tail				
Variable	pairs	Corr	Sig		Mean	SD	SE of Mean
SOCSTUD Social Studies					1.1285	.753	.145
	27	.568	.002				
SOCSTUD1					1.2059	.881	.170

Paired Differences			"				
Mean	SD	SE of Mean	"	t-value		df	2-tail Sig
-.0774	.768	.148	"	-.52		26	.605
99% CI (-.488, .333)			"				

t-tests for Paired Samples

	Number of		2-tail				
Variable	pairs	Corr	Sig		Mean	SD	SE of Mean
BASBATT Basic Battery					1.1240	.713	.094
	58	.596	.000				
BASBATT1					1.2174	.770	.101

Paired Differences			"				
Mean	SD	SE of Mean	"	t-value		df	2-tail Sig
-.0934	.668	.088	"	-1.06		57	.292
99% CI (-.327, .140)			"				

	Number of		2-tail				
Variable	pairs	Corr	Sig		Mean	SD	SE of Mean
COMBATT Complete Battery					1.1808	.733	.120
	37	.713	.000				
COMBATT1					1.2376	.779	.128

```
        Paired Differences        "
    Mean        SD   SE of Mean "    t-value              df      2-tail Sig
"""""""""""""""""""""""""""""""""""""""""""""""""""""""""""""""""""""""""""""""""
   -.0568        .574        .094 "      -.60                36           .551
  99% CI (-.313,  .200)          "
```

End of Appendix C.

References

Alaska Department of Education. (1984). *Summary of SRA testing for Centralized Correspondence Study April/May 1984*. Juneau, AK: Alaska Author.

Alaska Department of Education. (1985). *SRA survey of basic skills, Alaska Statewide Assessment, Spring of 1985*. Juneau, AK: Author.

Alaska Department of Education. (1986). *Results from 1981 CAT [for CCS]*. Juneau, AK: Author.

American Educational Research Association. (1995). *Annual meeting program, AERA, April 18-22, 1995, San Francisco [CA]*. Washington, DC: Author.

Audain, Tunya. (1987). Home education: The third option. *The Canadian School Executive*, April, 18-21, 24.

Batterbee, Gayla C. (1992). *The relationship of parent-child interactive systems to cognitive attributes in the home schooled child*. Doctoral dissertation, United States International University, San Diego, CA.

Bendell, Jean. (1987). *School's Out*. Bath, England: Ashgrove Press.

Blankenhorn, David. (1995). Fatherless America: Confronting our most urgent social problem. New York, NY: Basic Books (Harper Collins Publ.)

Bloom, Benjamin S. (1984, May). The search for methods of group instruction as effective as one-to-one tutoring. *Educational Leadership*, May, 1984, 4-17.

Blumenfeld, Samuel L. (1984). *N.E.A.: Trojan horse in American Education*. Boise, ID: The Paradigm Company.

Borg, W. R., & Gall, M. D. (1989). *Educational research: An introduction (5th ed.)*. New York, NY: Longman.

Breshears, Shirley Mae. (1996, May) *Characteristics of home schools and home school families in Idaho*. Unpublished doctoral dissertation. University of Idaho.

Buehrer, Eric. (1995). *The public orphanage: How public schools are making parents irrelevant*. Dallas, TX: Word Publishing.

Burns, Patrick C. (1993, December). A profile of selected characteristics of Arizona's home schooling families. Unpublished doctoral dissertation, Northern Arizona University.

Carson (Allie-Carson), Jayn. (1990). Structure and interaction patterns of home school families. *Home School Researcher*, *6*(3), 11-18.

Chatham-Carpenter, April. (1994). Home vs. public schoolers: Differing social opportunities. *Home School Researcher*, *10*(1), 15-24.

Churbuck, David C. (October 11, 1993). The ultimate school choice: No school at all. *Forbes*, 144, 145, 148-150.

Cizek, Gregory J. (1991). Alternative assessments: Promises and problems for home-based education policy. *Home School Researcher*, *7*(4), 13-21.

Cizek, Gregory J. (1993). The mismeasure of home schooling effectiveness: A commentary. *Home School Researcher*, *9*(3), 1-4.

Clark, Charles S. (1994). Home schooling: Is it a healthy alternative to public education? *The CQ [Congressional Quarterly] Researcher*, *4*(33), 769-792.

Clinton, Hillary Rodham. (1996). *It takes a village: And other lessons children teach us*. New York, NY: Simon & Schuster.

Coleman, James S. (1961). *The adolescent society*. Glencoe, IL: Free Press.

Coleman, James S., & Hoffer, Thomas. (1987). *Public and private high schools: The impact of communities*. New York, NY: Basic Books, Inc., Publishers.

Coleman, James S., Hoffer, Thomas, & Kilgore, Sally. (1982). *High school achievement: Public, Catholic, and private schools compared*. New York, NY: Basic Books.

Common, Ron W., & MacMullen, Marilyn. (1986). Home schooling... a growing movement. *Education Canada*, *26*(2), 4-7.

Delahooke, Mona Maarse. (1986). *Home educated children's social/emotional adjustment and academic achievement: A comparative study*. Unpublished doctoral dissertation, California School of Professional Psychology, Los Angeles, CA.

Donmoyer, Robert (Ed.). (1996). This issue: A focus on educational reform and the role of research in the reform process [special feature of the issue]. *Educational Researcher, 25*(7), 4-5.

Dorian, Terry, & Tyler, Zan. (1996). *Anyone can home school: How to find what works for you.* Lafayette, LA. Huntington House Publishers.

Duffy, Cathy. (1995). *Government nannies: The cradle-to-grave agenda of Goals 2000 and outcome based education.* Gresham, OR: Noble Publishing Associates.

Duvall, Steven F. (1994, August 30). *The effects of home education on children with learning disabilities.* A paper presented to the Home School Legal Defense Association, Paeonian Springs, VA.

Eagle Forum. (1996). NEA passes usual radical resolutions. *Education Reporter, 127,* 1, 2-4.

Falle, Bob. (1986). Standardized tests for home study students: Administration and results. *Method: Alaskan Perspectives, 7*(1), 22-24.

Famighetti, Robert. (1995). *The world almanac and book of facts, 1996.* Mahwah, NJ: World Almanac Books (of Funk & Wagnalls Corp.)

Farris, Michael P. (1996, October 12). *Keynote address.* Speech presented at the Annual National Christian Home Educators Leadership Conference, Dallas, TX.

Farris, Michael. (1990, October/November). Good enough to be left alone. *The Teaching Home, 8(*5), 37.

Fowler, Floyd J., Jr. (1988). *Survey research methods (revised edition).* Newbury Park, CA: SAGE Publications.

Frisbie, David. (1992). Book review. *Journal of Educational Measurement, 29*(2), 275.

Galloway, Rhonda A., & Sutton, Joe P. (1995). Home schooled and conventionally schooled high school graduates: A comparison of aptitude for and achievement in college English. *Home School Researcher, 11*(1), 1-9.

Good, R. (1984). A problem of multiple significance tests. *Journal of Research in Science Teaching, 21*(1), 105-106.

Good, Thomas L. & Brophy, Jere E. (1987). *Looking in classrooms (4th ed.)*. New York, NY: Harper & Row, Publishers.

Gordon, Edward E., & Gordon, Elaine H. (1990). *Centuries of tutoring: A history of alternative education in America and Western Europe*. Lanham, MD: University Press of America.

Growing Without Schooling. Available from Holt Associates, 2269 Massachusetts Ave., Cambridge MA 02140.

Gustafson, Sonia K. (1987). *A study of home schooling: Parental motivations and goals*. A senior thesis, Woodrow Wilson School of Public and International Affairs, Princeton University, Princeton, NJ.

Hagborg, Winston J. (1995). High school student television viewing time: A study of school performance and adjustment. *Child Study Journal, 25*(3), 155-167.

Havens, Joan Ellen. (1991). *A study of parent education levels as they relate to academic achievement among home schooled children*. Doctoral (Ed.D.) dissertation, Southwestern Baptist Theological Seminary, Fort Worth TX.

Hedin, Norma S. (1991). Self-concept of Baptist children in three educational settings. *Home School Researcher, 7*(3), 1-5.

Hirsch, E. D. (1996). *The schools we need and why we don't have them*. Garden City, NY: Doubleday.

Home School Court Report, The. Available from Home School Legal Defense Association, PO Box 159, Paeonian Springs VA 20129.

Home School Legal Defense Association. (1996, September/October). District of Columbia. *Home School Court Report, 12*(5), 9.

Hood, Mary E. (1991). Contemporary philosophical influences on the home schooling movement. *Home School Researcher, 7*(1), 1-8.

Hopkins, Kenneth D., Glass, Gene V., & Hopkins, B.R. (1987). *Basic statistics for the behavioral sciences (2nd ed.)*. Englewood Cliffs, NJ: Prentice-Hall, Inc.

Hopkins, Kenneth D., Stanley, Julian C., & Hopkins, B. R. (1990). *Educational and psychological measurement and evaluation (7th ed.)*. Englewood Cliffs, NJ: Prentice-Hall, Inc.

Hudson, Kathi. (1992). *Reinventing America's schools, Volumes 1 and 2: A practical guide to components of restructuring & non-traditional education.* Costa Mesa, CA: Citizens for Excellence in Education.

Hudson, Kathi. (1993). *Reinventing America's schools, Volumes 3: A practical guide to components of restructuring & non-traditional education.* Costa Mesa, CA: Citizens for Excellence in Education.

Hunter, John E., & Schmidt, Frank L. (1990). *Methods of meta-analysis: Correcting error and bias in research findings.* Newbury Park, CA: Sage Publications.

James, Kay C. (1996, February). Transforming America. *Imprimis, 25*(2), 1-5, 7.

Johnson, Kathie Carwile. (1991). Socialization practices of Christian home school educators in the state of Virginia. *Home School Researcher, 7(*1), 9-16.

Jones, Bob, III. (1991, June 3-7). Personal communication. Jones was resident Bob Jones University, Greenville, SC.

Kaseman, Larry, & Kaseman, Susan. (1991, January/February). Does homeschooling research help homeschooling? *Home Education Magazine,* 26-27, 46-49.

Kelley, Steven W. (1991). Socialization of home schooled children: A self-concept study. *Home School Researcher, 7*(4), 1-12.

Klicka, Christopher J. (1993). *The right choice: The incredible failure of public education and the rising hope of home schooling (rev. ed.).*Gresham, Oregon: Noble Publishing Associates.

Klicka, Christopher J. (1996, February). *Home schooling in the United States: A legal analysis.* Paeonian Springs, VA: Home School Legal Defense Association.

Knowles, J. Gary, & Muchmore, James A. (1995). Yep! We're grown-up home-school kids C and we're doing just fine, thank you. *Journal of Research on Christian Education, 4*(1), 35-56.

Knowles, J. Gary, Mayberry, Maralee, & Ray, Brian D. (1991, December 24). *An assessment of home schools in Nevada, Oregon, Utah, and Washington: Implications for public education and a vehicle for informed policy decision, summary report*. A report to the United States Department of Education, Field Initiated Research Project Grant #R117E90220.

Larson, R. W. (1983). Adolescents' daily experience with family and friends: Contrasting opportunity systems. *Journal of Marriage and Family, 45,* 739-750.

Lewis, Terry. (1985). *School on trial: A positive alternative.* Vital, Manitoba, Canada: Christian School Consultants.

Lieberman, Myron. (1989). Privatization and educational choice. New York, NY: St. Martin's Press.

Lieberman, Myron. (1993). *Public education: An autopsy.* Cambridge, MA: Harvard University Press.

Lines, Patricia M. (1991, October). *Estimating the home schooled population (working paper OR 91-537).* Washington DC: Office of Educational Research and Improvement, U.S. Department of Education.

Lines, Patricia M. (1994, February). Homeschooling: Private choices and public obligations. *Home School Researcher, 10*(3), 9-26.

Lines, Patricia M. (1996, October). Home schooling comes of age. *Educational Leadership, 54*(2), 63-67.

Martin, Jane R. (1992). *The schoolhome: Rethinking schools for changing families.* Cambridge, MA: Harvard University Press.

Mayberry, Maralee. (1988*). Doing it their way: A study of Oregon's home schoolers.* Doctoral dissertation, University of Oregon, Eugene.

Mayberry, Maralee, Knowles, J. Gary, Ray, Brian D., & Marlow, Stacey. (1995). *Home schooling: Parents as educators.* Newbury Park, CA: Corwin Press (of Sage Publ.).

Medlin, Richard G. (1994). Predictors of academic achievement in home educated children: Aptitude, self-concept, and pedagogical practices. *Home School Researcher, 10*(3), 1-7.

Microsoft, (1994). *Microsoft Excel (Version 5.0).* Redmond, WA: Author.

Mitchell, James V. (1983). *Tests in print III.* Lincoln, NE: University of Nebraska Press.

Mitchell, James V., Jr. (1985). *The ninth mental measurements yearbook.* Lincoln, NE: The Buros Institute of Mental Measurements.

Montgomery, Linda R. (1989). The effect of home schooling on the leadership skills of home schooled students. *Home School Researcher*, 5(1), 1-10.

Nash, Ronald H. (1990).*The closing of the American Heart : What's really wrong with America's schools*. Dallas, TX: Probe Books.

National Association of Elementary School Principals. (1989-1990). *Platform 1989-1990*. Author: Alexandria, VA.

National Association of State Boards of Education. (1994, January). Home schooling. *Policy Update*, 2(2), 1-2.

National Commission on Excellence in Education, The. (1983). *A nation at risk: The imperative for educational reform*. Washington, DC: U. S. Government Printing Office.

National Education Association. (1990). *The 1990-91 resolutions of the National Education Association*. Washington, DC: Author.

National School Safety Center News Service, Pepperdine University. (1991). *Annual study shows 3 million crimes on school campuses*. Malibu, CA: Author.

Oliveira (de Oliveira), Paulo C. M., Watson, Timothy G., & Sutton, Joe P. (1994). Differences in critical thinking skills among students educated in public schools, Christian schools, and home schools, by. *Home School Researcher*, 10(4), 1-8.

Oregon Department of Education, Office of Student Services. (1993, May 14). *Number of registered home schooling students compared with number of tested home schooling students 1986-1992*. Salem, OR: Author.

Oregon Department of Education, Office of Student Services. (1996). *Home school statistics, 1995-96*. Salem, OR: Author.

Perelman, Lewis J. (1992). *School's out: A radical new formula for the revitalization of America's educational system*. New York, NY: Avon Books.

Popenoe, David. (1996). *Life without father: Compelling new evidence that fatherhood and marriage are indispensable for the good of children and society*. New York, NY: Martin Kessler Books, The Free Press.

Priesnitz, Wendy, & Priesnitz, Heidi. (1990, March). *Home-based education in Canada: An investigation.* Unionville, Ontario, Canada: The Alternative Press.

Rakestraw, Jennie F. (1987). *An analysis of home schooling for elementary school-age children in Alabama.* Doctoral dissertation, University of Alabama, Tuscaloosa.

Rakestraw, Jennie F. (1988). Home schooling in Alabama. *Home School Researcher, 4*(4), 1-6.

Ray, Brian D. (1988, August 12). The kitchen classroom. *Christianity Today, 32*(11), 23-26.

Ray, Brian D. (1989). Understanding public, private, and home school students' beliefs, attitudes, and intentions related to science learning. *Home School Researcher, 5*(3), 1-11.

Ray, Brian D. (1990a). *Home education in Montana: Family characteristics and student achievement.* (Available from the National Home Education Research Institute, PO Box 13939, Salem OR 97309.)

Ray, Brian D. (1990b). *A nationwide study of home education: Family characteristics, legal matters, and student achievement.* (Available from the National Home Education Research Institute, PO Box 13939, Salem OR 97309.)

Ray, Brian D. (1990c). *Social capital, value consistency, and the achievement outcomes of home education.* A paper presented at the Annual Meeting of the American Educational Research Association, April 16-20, Boston, MA. (Available from the National Home Education Research Institute, PO Box 13939, Salem OR 97309.)

Ray, Brian D. (1991). *Home education in North Dakota: Family characteristics and student achievement.* (Available from the National Home Education Research Institute, PO Box 13939, Salem OR 97309.)

Ray, Brian D. (1992a). *Home education in Oklahoma: Family characteristics, student achievement, and policy matters.* (Available from the National Home Education Research Institute, PO Box 13939, Salem OR 97309.)

Ray, Brian D. (1992b). *Marching to the beat of their own drum: A profile of home education research.* Paeonian Springs, VA: Home School Legal Defense Association. (Available from the

National Home Education Research Institute, PO Box 13939, Salem OR 97309.)

Ray, Brian D. (1993). Home education revitalized. In Thomas C. Hunt & James C. Carper (Eds.), *Religious schools in the United States, K-12: A source book.* New York, NY: Garland Publishing, Inc.

Ray, Brian D. (1994). *A nationwide study of home education in Canada: Family characteristics, student achievement, and other topics.* . (Available from the National Home Education Research Institute, PO Box 13939, Salem OR 97309.)

Ray, Brian D. (1995). *Learning at home in Montana: Student achievement and family characteristics.* (Available from the National Home Education Research Institute, PO Box 13939, Salem OR 97309.)

Ray, Brian D. (1996). *Home education research fact sheet IIb.* (Available from the National Home Education Research Institute, PO Box 13939, Salem OR 97309.)

Richman, Howard B., Girten, William, & Snyder, Jay. (1990). Academic achievement and its relationship to selected variables among Pennsylvania homeschoolers. *Home School Researcher,* 6(4), 9-16.

Richman, Sheldon. (1994). *Separating school and state: How to liberate America's families.* Fairfax, VA: The Future of Freedom Foundation.

Russell, Terry. (1994). Cross-validation of a multivariate path analysis of predictors of home school student academic achievement. *Home School Researcher,* 10(1), 1-13.

Sanchez, Miguel. (April 1996). Personal communication. Sanchez was director of admissions, Nyack College, Nyack, NY.

Shavelson, Richard J. (1988). *Statistical reasoning for the behavioral sciences (2nd ed.).* Boston, MA: Allyn and Bacon.

Shyers, Larry E. (1992). A comparison of social adjustment between home and traditionally schooled students. *Home School Researcher,* 8(3), 1-8.

Smedley, Thomas C. Socialization of home school children. (1992). *Home School Researcher,* 8(3), 9-16.

Smith, Thomas Ewin. (1992). Time use and change in academic achievement: A longitudinal follow-up. *Journal of Youth and Adolescence, 21*(6), 725-747.

Snow, Catherine E., Barnes, Wendy S., Chandler, Jean, Goodman, Irene F., & Hemphill, Lowry. (1991). *Unfulfilled expectations: Home and school influences on literacy.* Cambridge, MA: Harvard University Press.

Somerville, Scott. (1996, December 10). Personal. Somerville was an attorney for Home School Legal Defense Association, Paeonian Springs, VA.

Sowell, Thomas. (1993). *Inside American education: The decline, the deception, the dogmas.* New York, NY: The Free Press.

Sprinthall, Richard C. (1990). *Basic statistical analysis (3rd ed.).* Englewood Cliffs, NJ: Prentice-Hall, Inc.

SPSS, Inc. (1995). *SPSS for Windows (Version 6.1.2).* Chicago, IL: Author.

Stecklow, Steve. (1994, May 10). Fed up with schools, more parents turn to teaching them at home. *The Wall Street Journal, 130*(91), A1, A12.

Stockard, Jean, & Mayberry, Maralee. (1992). *Effective educational environments.* Newbury Park, CA: Corwin Press (of Sage Publ.).

Tamayo, Lincoln. (1990, November 28). Personal communication. Tamayo was assistant to the vice president enrollment management, Boston University, Boston, MA.

Taylor, John Wesley, 5th. (1986, June). Self-concept in home-schooling children. *Home School Researcher, 2*(2), 1-3.

Taylor, Lesley Ann. (1993). *At home in school: A qualitative inquiry into three Christian home schools.* Doctoral dissertation, Stanford University, Stanford, CA.

Teaching Home, The. Available from PO Box 20219, Portland OR 97220-0219.

Tennessee Department of Education. (1988). *Tennessee statewide averages, home school student test results, Stanford Achievement Test, grades 2, 5, 7 and 9.* Nashville, TN: Author.

Tillman, Vicki D. (1995). Home schoolers, self-esteem, and socialization. *Home School Researcher, 11*(3), 1-6.

Toch, Thomas. (1991a, December 9). The exodus [from public schools]. *U.S. News & World Report, 111*(24), 66-68, 71-74, 76,77.

Toch, Thomas. (1991b). *In the name of excellence: The struggle to reform the nation's schools, why it's failing, and what should be done.* New York, NY: Oxford University Press.

Treat, Elizabeth Baurle. (1990). Parents teaching reading and writing at home: An ethnographic study. *Home School Researcher, 6*(2), 9-19.

Tyack, David B. (1974). *The one best system: A history of American urban education.* Cambridge, MA: Harvard University Press.

United States Bureau of the Census. (1994a). School enrollment—social and economic characteristics of students: October 1994; Table A-5. *Current population report P20-487.* Washington, DC: Author.

United States Bureau of the Census. (1994b). *Statistical abstract of the United States 1994 (114th edition).* Washington, DC: Author.

United States Bureau of the Census. (1996a). *Current population reports, series P60; table F-7.* Washington, DC: Author.

United States Bureau of the Census. (1996b). *Current population survey, March 1996 (Table entitled: Persons aged 25 and over by educational attainment).* Washington, DC: Author.

United States Department of Education, National Center for Education Statistics. (1992). *National education longitudinal study of 1988 [NELS 88], second follow-up, parent questionnaire.* Washington, DC: Author.

United States Department of Education, National Center for Education Statistics. (1996). *Statistics in brief, June 1996; Revenues and expenditures for public elementary and secondary education: School year 1993-94. [From: Common core of data: National public education financial survey.* Washington, DC: Author.

United States Department of Education, Office of Educational Research and Improvement. (1992). *NAEP [National Assessment of Educational Progress] data on disk: 1992 almanac viewer.* Washington, DC: Author.

United States Department of Education, Office of Educational Research and Improvement. (1993, October). *Projections of education statistics to 2004.* Washington, DC: Author.

United States Department of Education, Office of Educational Research and Improvement. (1995). *The pocket condition of education, 1995.* Washington, DC: Author.

United States Department of Education, Office of Educational Research and Improvement. (1996a). *National Education Longitudinal Study [NELS 88]: 1988-94; data files and electronic codebook system (CD-ROM).* Washington, DC: Author.

United States Department of Education, Office of Educational Research and Improvement. (1996b, May). *National Education Longitudinal Study 1988-94: Descriptive summary report.* Washington, DC: Author.

Van Galen, Jane A. (1988). Ideology, curriculum, and pedagogy in home education. *Education and Urban Society, 21*(1), 52-68.

Wartes, Jon. (1987). Report from the 1986 home school testing and other descriptive information about Washington's home schoolers: a summary. *Home School Researcher, 3*(1), 1-4.

Wartes, Jon. (1988). Summary of two reports from the Washington Home School Research Project, 1987. *Home School Researcher, 4*(2), 1-4.

Wartes, Jon. (1989). *Report from the 1988 Washington homeschool testing.* (Available from the Washington Homeschool Research Project at 16109 NE 169 Pl., Woodinville, WA, 98072).

Wartes, Jon. (1990a, September). *The relationship of selected input variables to academic achievement among Washington's homeschoolers.* (Available from the Washington Homeschool Research Project at 16109 N. E. 169 Pl., Woodinville, WA, 98072).

Wartes, Jon. (1990b, September). *Report from the 1986 through 1989 Washington homeschool testing.* (Available from the Washington Homeschool Research Project at 16109 N. E. 169 Pl., Woodinville, WA, 98072).

Washington State Superintendent of Public Instruction. (1985). *Washington State's experimental programs using the parent as tutor under the supervision of a Washington State certificated teacher* 1984-1985. Olympia, WA: Author.

Webb, Julie. (1990). *Children learning at home*. England, and Bristol, PA, USA: Falmer Press.

Williams, P., Haertel, E., Haertel, G., & Walberg, H. (1982). The impact of leisure time television on school learning. *American Educational Research Journal*, 19, 19-50.

Wright, Cheryl. (1988, November). Home school research: Critique and suggestions for the future. *Education and Urban Society*, *21*(1), 96-113.

Index

—A—

Academic learning time, 96
Achievement, academic, ix, xii, xiii,
  3, 4, 7, 8, 9, 10, 11, 12, 16, 17,
  21, 22, 23, 24, 25, 54, 55, 56, 57,
  58, 59, 60, 61, 62, 63, 64, 65, 66,
  68, 70, 78, 79, 80, 81, 82, 84, 86,
  91, 92, 93, 95, 97, 98, 99, 100,
  101, 116, 118, 119, 120, 121,
  122, 124, 125, 128, 129, 130,
  132, 134, 135, 136, 138
Adulthood, 13, 96
Ameliorate, 99
Assumptions, 5

—C—

Certification, teacher, xii, xiii, 5, 11,
  16, 22, 23, 30, 58, 59, 74, 98,
  101
Commentary, 71, 85, 128
Computer, xiii, 4, 23, 29, 51, 65,
  74, 78, 82, 84, 93, 99, 120
Conclusions, ix, 25
Cost, 68, 73, 83
Curriculum, xii, 4, 6, 16, 17, 23, 49,
  53, 64, 68, 69, 73, 77, 81, 84, 96,
  138

—D—

Definitions, 16, 66
Delimitations, 25
Demographics, xii, 3, 16, 24, 27, 75

—E—

Education level of parent, xiii, 23,
  24, 58, 59, 60, 61, 62, 63, 68, 80,
  83, 100, 130
Education level, of parent, xiii, 23,
  24, 58, 59, 60, 61, 62, 63, 68, 80,
  83, 100, 130

—G—

Gender, xiii, 23, 58, 59, 60, 61, 62,
  80, 99, 100
Grade, 8, 10, 45, 54, 73, 75, 78, 84
Graduates of home schooling, xi,
  68, 83, 129

—H—

Hypothesis, 22, 100

—I—

Income, xii, xiii, 12, 23, 24, 28, 30,
  58, 59, 68, 72, 76, 83, 91, 93, 99
Instrument, 15, 16, 18, 19, 51, 104

—L—

Legal status, xiii, 16, 23, 29, 58, 59
Library, xiii, 23, 24, 28, 59, 60, 68,
  74, 80, 84, 88, 99
Limitations, 12, 25, 26, 85, 91
Longitudinal, xii, 3, 12, 15, 16, 26,
  136, 137

—M—

Methodology, x, xi, 15, 28, 31, 88

—O—

Occupation, of parents, 28

—P—

Population, xii, 2, 3, 5, 8, 12, 17, 26, 29, 72, 76, 84, 132, 137
Population, target, xii, 17
Predictor variables, xiii, 23, 58, 59, 60, 61, 62, 63, 65, 66, 79, 81, 92, 123

—R—

Race, 28, 45, 74, 75, 99, 100
Regression, 23, 58, 60, 61, 62, 63, 79
Regulation by the state, xiii, 23, 63, 64, 81, 101
Regulation, by the state, xiii, 23, 63, 64, 81, 101
Religion, xii, 18, 31, 34, 35, 68, 73, 83, 87, 94, 98, 99
Response rate, 20, 85

Responsibility, 88, 90

—S—

Sample, 3, 12, 17, 18, 19, 20, 25, 29, 30, 31, 47, 55, 56, 69, 70, 71, 75, 76, 84, 85, 116, 118
Social capital, 87, 93, 134
Socialization, xii, xiii, 2, 3, 7, 9, 10, 12, 20, 25, 49, 54, 55, 65, 68, 77, 79, 82, 84, 85, 86, 87, 88, 89, 91, 92, 93, 97, 98, 101, 127, 128, 130, 135, 136, 137
Society, 2, 88, 91, 100, 102, 128, 133
Strengths, v, ix, x, 85, 143

—T—

Test administrator, 54
Tutoring, 28, 94, 95, 96, 127, 130, 139

—V—

Value community, 94
Value consistency, 94, 134
Village, 88, 90, 128

Order Form for

Strengths of Their Own —
Home Schoolers Across America

Academic Achievement, Family Characteristics, and Longitudinal Traits

You may order more copies of *Strengths of Their Own—Home Schoolers Across America* using this form.

Name: _____

Street Address: _____

City, State, Zip: _____

Phone Number: _____

Number of Copies _____ x $19.95 each = $_____

Shipping/Handling: No. Copies _____ x $2.00 = $_____

TOTAL Enclosed U.S.$_____

Make check payable to "NHERI" and send to:

National Home Education Research Institute
PO Box 13939
925 Cottage Street NE
Salem, Oregon 97309 U.S.A.
    tel. (503) 364-1490
    fax (503) 364-2827
    World Wide Web Site http://www.nheri.org
    e-mail: mail@nheri.org

Publications Available from the
National Home Education Research Institute

Home School Researcher (1985-present) – a quarterly, refereed, scholarly journal; an index and back issues are available

Marching to the Beat of Their Own Drum: A Profile of Home Education Research (1992) – excellent review of many topics of research

Home Centered Learning Annotated Bibliography (1997, revised regularly) – over 1,000 references, paper copy and on computer diskette

Strengths of Their Own—Home Schoolers Across America: Academic Achievement, Family Characteristics, and Longitudinal Traits (1997) — scholarly **book** by Brian D. Ray, Ph.D.

At Home in School: A Qualitative Inquiry into Three Christian Home Schools (1993)

A Nationwide Study of Home Education in Canada: Family Characteristics, Student Achievement, and Other Topics (1994)

A Nationwide Study of Home Education: Family Characteristics, Legal Matters, and Student Achievement (1990), done in the United States

What Research Says About Home Schooling **Video**, professionally produced (1993)

Oregon Home School Research Report (1995)

Home Education in Oklahoma: Family Characteristics, Student Achievement, and Policy Matters (1992)

Learning at Home in North Dakota: Family Attributes and Student Achievement (1993)

A Brief Statistical Analysis of Academic Achievement Test Data from Home Educated Students Operating Under the Virginia Religious Exemption Statute (1994)

Home Education in Montana: Family Characteristics and Student Achievement (1990)

A Brief Statistical Analysis of Academic Achievement Test Data from Home Educated Students in Florida (1994)

Home Education in North Dakota: Family Characteristics and Student Achievement (1991)

A Brief Statistical Analysis of Academic Achievement Test Data from Students in Maine's Home-Based Non-Approved Private Schools (1994)

Oregon Home Education (1993)

A Nationwide Study of Home Education in Canada: Family Characteristics, Student Achievement, and Other Topics (A Synopsis), two-color summary of full-length report mentioned above (1994)

Religious Orthodoxy and Student Achievement in Home Education (1991)
Home Schooling, Science Achievement, and Parents' Beliefs About God and the Origin of Species and Life (1991)
A Review of Home School Research: Characteristics of the Families and Learner Outcomes (1990)
A Comparison of Home Schooling and Conventional Schooling: With a Focus on Learner Outcomes (1986)
An Overview of Home Schooling in the United States: Its Growth and Development and Future Challenges (1989)
Setting the Context for State Regulation of Home-Schooling Parents (1989)
Social Capital, Value Consistency, and the Learner Outcomes of Home Education (1990)
Beliefs, Attitudes, and Intentions of Science Learners in Public, Private, and Home Schools (1990)
Review of Home Education Research (1990) – reprint from a magazine article
Home schools: A Synthesis of Research on Characteristics and Learner Outcomes, reprint from research journal
Home Schooling: Parents as Educators (1995), scholarly **book** by Drs. Maralee Mayberry, J. Gary Knowles, Brian Ray, and Stacey Marlow
Home Schooling: Political, Historical, and Pedagogical Perspectives (1991), scholarly **book** edited by Drs. Jane A. Van Galen & Mary A. Pitman
Home Education Research Fact Sheet Ib – A one-page summary of studies that makes about 15 statements
Home Education Research Fact Sheet IIb – A one-page summary with information in addition to that in *Sheet I*
Home Education Research Fact Sheet IIIb – A one-page summary that builds on fact sheets I and II.

For more information, including a catalog with prices, contact:

National Home Education Research Institute
P.O. Box 13939
Salem, Oregon 97309
phone (503) 364-1490   facsimile (503) 364-2827
e-mail: mail@nheri.org   Web Site: www.nheri.org